the Milltowns
a family reunion

the Milltowns
a family reunion

Sergio Benedetti

NATIONAL GALLERY OF IRELAND
DUBLIN 1997

Published to accompany the exhibition *The Milltowns: a family reunion* at the National Gallery of Ireland 22 October - 15 December 1997

Copyright © 1997 Sergio Benedetti, the Contributors and the National Gallery of Ireland
All rights reserved

ISBN 0903-162-44X

A catalogue record for this publication is available from the British Library

Published by the National Gallery of Ireland
Edited by Fionnuala Croke
Designed and produced by Creative Inputs
Printed by Nicholson & Bass

Cover: Pompeo Batoni, *Joseph Leeson later 1st Earl of Milltown*, 1744, no. 7

Contents

Foreword by Raymond Keaveney — vi

Introduction by Sergio Benedetti — viii

Author's Acknowledgements — x

Genealogy — xii

the Milltowns by Sergio Benedetti — 1

the Portraits — 11

the Caricature by Sergio Benedetti — 37

the Caricatures — 39

the Statues in the Colonnades at Russborough by Chris Caffrey — 67

the Taste — 77

Russborough - its decoration and furniture, some preliminary thoughts by the Knight of Glin — 119

Bibliography — 134

Index

Foreword

When the National Gallery of Ireland was established in 1854 it gave public expression to what had long been a private passion, namely the collection of works of art. Up until the foundation of the Gallery, the general public had only modest access to works of art by way of visiting churches and public buildings. Wealthy individuals, by contrast, enjoyed the fine arts which decorated their elegant homes and the residences of their friends. Such collections were built up over generations, with much of the most intense collecting dating to the mid-eighteenth century, the high point of the Grand Tour, when wealthy individuals travelled to the continent and especially to Italy and Rome to finish their education and do some serious shopping.

Among the most distinguished Irish families to undertake the Grand Tour and commission and collect works of art for their Irish residences was the Leeson family, who were ennobled in 1763 as Earls of Milltown. During the early part of the century the family's home was located on St Stephen's Green, close to the centre of Dublin, where they operated a profitable brewery out of an adjacent property. In the 1730s Joseph Leeson acquired lands in Co. Wicklow close to the river Liffey, at what is now known as Russborough, where he proceeded to construct a great country house to function as his main residence. His two documented visits to Italy (1744-45 and 1750-51), and the subsequent travels of his descendants, served to provide a wealth of art works to decorate the fine interiors of Richard Castle's great Palladian mansion and the family's town house on St Stephen's Green. These acquisitions were complemented by a rich variety of art works and furnishings commissioned from local artists and craftsmen. In 1899, Geraldine, Dowager Countess of Milltown, determined that the contents of Russborough be gifted to the National Gallery, a gift finalised in 1902. Such was the extent of this act of patronage that a new wing needed to be added to the original Gallery building to accommodate the paintings, sculpture, furniture, silverware and library. In acknowledgement of this exceptional gift the centre wing of the Gallery (1903) is referred to as the Milltown Wing.

This exhibition, organised by Sergio Benedetti, who is also responsible for the writing of the catalogue, pays homage to the Milltown family and its marvellous contribution to the history and excellence of this institution. It places particular emphasis on providing us with a series of family portraits, both formal and informal, which were commissioned from artists such as Batoni, Lee, Reynolds and Pier Leone Ghezzi. In addition there is a small selection of works which reflect the taste of the period by way of antique pieces, bronzes, sculpture, furnishings and paintings.

In putting this exhibition together we are indebted to the many individuals and institutions who agreed to making their treasures available for display. Thanks must also be extended to Douglas Bennett, Chris Caffrey and the Knight of Glin who have contributed to the catalogue

Raymond Keaveney
Director
National Gallery of Ireland

Introduction

Exactly one hundred years ago a member of the National Gallery of Ireland made the first contact with the Milltown Collection. At the time nothing was known of the treasures of Russborough. The residence of the Earls of Milltown was kept strictly private and access was limited to a select number of people. On 21 October 1897 this permission was unexpectedly granted by Geraldine Countess of Milltown to Walter Amstrong, third Director of the Gallery, with precise instructions: 'There is a train that leaves Terenure at twenty minutes past eight o'clock and another at eleven o'clock a.m. which will take you to Featherbed Lane, where I will have a man waiting to open the gate for you'. As we know today, as a result of this encounter and of many subsequent long and difficult discussions, the Gallery received what could be claimed as one of the most important collections of works of art from the Grand Tour. The reasons which motivated this donation were enunciated five years later in the Act of Indenture between Lady Milltown and the Gallery Board. The Countess was the widow of the 6th Earl and with no direct line of descent, she decided to leave the collection to the Gallery as a memorial to her late husband, if appropriate accommodation could be provided and on condition that it should be kept intact and together. As an immediate consequence a new wing was built which practically doubled the Gallery space and in 1906 the collection was opened to the public.

Regrettably, after the death of the Countess, her wishes were not completely fulfilled and although the core of the paintings never left the Gallery, the permanent loan of pictures and furniture to State offices, and books and silver to other national institutions was allowed. In the meantime Russborough changed owners several times until 1952 when Sir Alfred Beit, rescuing the mansion from an otherwise uncertain destiny, purchased it and, as we know, once more filled its handsome rooms with masterpieces.

The idea for this exhibition began in December 1996 when, having informed us of his munificent bequest, Sir Denis Mahon offered to lend us his small *Portrait of a Lady Leeson*, painted by Batoni, for an exhibition which would include all the other Milltown portraits already in the Gallery. From the initial proposition of a 'family reunion' the project gradually grew, as frequently happens. The approaching anniversary of a hundred years from the moment the Gallery became aware of the collection seemed the appropriate opportunity to celebrate also the generosity of the gift and the artistic patronage of that family, and it was then decided to add two more sections to the show dedicated to the 'caricature' and to the 'taste'.

Since the Collection was largely created by the first two Earls, the research essentially focused on their lives, their ambitions and their circle of friends. Remarkably, for a family of such wealth and notoriety, not a single autograph letter has been found, and all the available records, excluding some legal documents, were reported by their contemporaries. I considered this information very important, like the works of art purchased, in providing a more complete picture of their lifestyle, even if this has resulted in the inclusion of very long end notes.

In making the selection for this exhibition my primary concern was to present paintings, sculptures and *objets d'art* never seen before or not usually seen by the public. Therefore, many notable Baroque canvases were excluded because they are currently on permanent display in the Gallery rooms.

A brilliant input to the catalogue was made by The Knight of Glin and Chris Caffrey with their more recent research on the subject, and Douglas Bennet generously offered his expertise in his specific field.

The findings of this study have brought many unexpected results but they are only part of a survey which is not yet concluded. With my fellow contributors I believe that now, with the past mistakes amended, further examination and investigation is needed and perhaps only then will we have a full understanding of the quality and richness of this remarkable eighteenth-century Irish collection which, regrettably, is the only one of such entity which still survives in the country.

Sergio Benedetti
September 1997

Author's Acknowledgements

This exhibition would not have been possible without the generosity of a few key lenders both private and public. I would particularly like to thank Lady Beit, Lord Cavendish of Furness, Sir Denis Mahon, Sir Roy Strong, the Walters Art Gallery, the Yale Centre for British Art and the Philadelphia Museum of Art.

I am also very grateful for the assistance received from a number of distinguished people, The Earl of Meath, Francis D. Murnaghan, The Earl and Countess of Dunraven, Lord Shelbourne, William Finlay, Mrs. West, Christopher Foley, Donald Galt, James and Therese Gorry, Deirdre Rowsome and Donald MacDonnell. My task would have not been achieved if it had not been supported by several departments of my Gallery and in particular by Nieves Fernandez, Marie Fitzgerald, Niamh Gogan, Roy Hewson, Marie McFeely, Niamh McGuinne, Maighread McParland, Andrew O'Connor and Susan O'Connor.

I received valuable assistance from many Institutions, like the Library of the National Gallery of London, the Courtald Institute of Art Library, the Witt Library, the Paul Mellon Centre for studies in British Art, the Walpole S. Lewis Library, the Rhode Island School of Design, The Metropolitan Museum of Art, l'Istituto Nazionale per la Grafica, the National Portrait Gallery, London, the Scottish National Portrait Gallery, The National Trust and the National Trust for Scotland.

Throughout the catalogue I have relied upon the help of many scholar-friends, and I thank these beginning with Edgar Peters Bowron, Richard Charlton-Jones, Luigi Ficacci, Gabriele Finaldi, John Ingamells, Alastair Laing, Adrian Le Harivel, Nicholas Penny, Michael Wynne, and in particular Douglas Bennet, Chris Caffery and the Knight of Glin for their generous response and valuable contribution.

My greatest debt is to Fionnuala Croke who took on her shoulders the responsibility of editing this catalogue and of coordinating the incoming loans to the exhibition.

Finally, a special thanks to the late Sir Alfred Beit and to Lady Beit for preserving Russborough for our present and future appreciation.

Detail of Joseph Leeson *later* 1st Earl of Milltown (1711?-1783)

JOSEPH LEESON (1660 - 1741) > 1695 Margaret Brice daughter of Andrew Brice Sheriff of Dublin

Rev. Robert Henry, *Presbyterian Minister in Dublin*

3 Martha >1741 Richard Cooke of Cookesborough, Co. Westmeath

4 Mary

5 Joyce >1721 Sir Robert Blackwood of Ballyleidy, Co. Down

6 Margaret (d.um. 1742)

Anne >1717 *Hugh Henry of Straffan M.P. for Antrim* (d.1743)

1 *Joseph>1764 Lady Catherine Rawdon daughter of John 1st Earl of Moira*

JOSEPH LEESON 1ST EARL (1711 - 1783)

> 1729 Cecilia Leigh of Rathangan Co. Kildare (d.1737)

> 1739 Anne Preston (1720/1-1766) daughter of Nathaniel Preston of Swainstown Co. Meath

4 Anne (b.1750) > 1770 *2 Hugh Henry of Lodge Park Co. Kildare*

> 1768 Elizabeth French (d.1842) daughter of the Very Rev. William French, Dean of Armagh

5 William (1770-1819) >1796 Mary daughter of Robert Buchanan

6 Cecilia>1789 David La Touche

7 Frances Arabella (-1840) >1790 Marcus Beresford

8 Robert (1773-1850) 1st>1795 Grace daughter of Michael Head 2ndly>1834 Harriet sister of Sir Henry Brooke

JOSEPH 2ND EARL (1730-1801) d.um.

3 Mary>1784 John Lord Naas, later 2nd Earl of Mayo (d.s.p. 1809)

BRICE 3RD EARL (1735 - 1807) > 1765 Maria Graydon daughter of John Graydon

1 Joseph (1766-1800) > 1798 Emily Douglas who m. 2ndly 2nd Baron Cloncurry

2 John (1767-1835) >1793 Martha daughter of Rev. John Ryley

3

2 Henry Talbot (1800-1829)

3 Cecilia Charlotte (d.1819)

JOSEPH 4TH EARL (1799 - 1866) > 1828 Barbara (d.1874) daughter of Joshua Colles Meredyth

JOSEPH HENRY 5TH EARL (1829-1871) d.um.

EDWARD NUGENT 6TH EARL (1835-1890)

HENRY 7TH EARL (1837-1891) d.um.

4 (twin) Barbara Emily Maria (d.1903) >1864 Lt. Gen. G. G. Chetwynd-Stapylton

5 (twin) Cecilia Maria (d.1903) >1856 Major Edmund Henry Turton

> 1871 Lady Geraldine Evelyn Stanhope (d. 1914) daughter of the 5th Earl of Harrington

the Milltowns

Sergio Benedetti

The son of a brewer created a P[ee]r,
Wine makes L[or]ds, I've been told,
and pray why should not beer ? *

The Leeson family appears to have originated in Northamptonshire and from different sources we learn that their settlement in Ireland took place in the second half of the seventeenth century.[1] Hugh Leeson, the first to be properly documented, was a sergeant in the army of Charles II and after he had spent a while in the Dublin Militia he left to begin the brewery business which was to bring prosperity and nobility to his heirs. In 1664 he was already the owner of a Lot no. 5 in South St Stephen's Green, at the time just a garden suburb. With the fast development of the area, he built his residence and the brewery there and that side of the Green soon became known as 'Leeson's Walk'. Nothing more is known of him except that he was buried in 1700 in the holy ground of the Church of St Peter and St Kevin.

Hugh's only son, named Joseph, continued as his principal business to be a brewer although he showed an uncommon ability also as a real estate investor which earned him strong criticism from Jonathan Swift.[2] However, such disapproval, even from the famous Dean of St Patrick, did not prevent him increasing his wealth and forming, in 1695, a very advantageous marriage with the heiress of the Dublin Alderman Andrew Brice. With this success he then tried to obtain a grant of arms from the heraldic authority, while his properties in St Stephen's Green alone amounted to five sites.[3] In one of these, no. 82 of the south side, he had his family residence, while in the vast gardens to the rear he kept his big brewery, and that land was known as 'Leeson's Fields'.[4]

It is not clear how many children he had because several died as infants,[5] and equally unclear is the birth date of his first and only surviving son, called after him Joseph.[6] While the father was careful in choosing the most appropriate society for his daughters, we must imagine also that nothing was spared in the education of the young Joseph to make of him a real gentleman. In 1729, Joseph Junior married Cecilia Leigh. She bore him three children, two sons and one daughter. The two sons afterwards became the 2nd and the 3rd Earls of Milltown. The marriage was not a happy union and, according to Letitia Pilkington the playwright, the complete responsibility lay with the husband: '… I remember the deplorable Condition to which he reduced his first Wife', Pilkington recalled, 'who died of his Love, as did his Child, the Nurse it was given to, and her Husband'.[7] Cecilia died in 1737, and just one month later Joseph wed again. This time the name of the bride was Anne Preston. She was young and rich and most of all she had important relatives.[8]

In 1741 Joseph the brewer died leaving a huge inheritance to Joseph Junior. An estate of £50,000 in money, and £6,000 per annum income.[9] With this fortune Joseph was able to give immediate shape to his ambitious plans. He purchased a large property in County Wicklow which included the townland of Russellstown with its sub-denomination of Russellsborough, better known today as Russborough, and commissioned the construction of a new country mansion designed by Richard Cassels (or Castle) with the possible assistance of Francis Bindon.[10] The brewery in the meantime was leased to someone else for thirty-one years.[11] His next step was to acquire a seat in the Irish House of Commons, and in 1743 he became a Member of Parliament for Rathcormick (Rathcormack, Co. Cork).[12]

The building work of the country house took many years to complete and although between Dublin and London the life of Joseph Leeson appears not to have been deprived of excitement, he decided to undertake his Grand Tour.[13] Like many other gentlemen, the purpose of his journey to Italy was to acquire taste and sophistication through the direct observation of the antiquities of that country, but also to secure a sufficient number of works of art for his new residence in Wicklow. In Rome, where he stayed for many months, he sat for Pompeo Batoni for a three-quarter-length portrait (no. 7) and purchased four landscapes from Giovanni Paolo Panini (nos. 37-40). At the beginning of 1745 an episode occurred which precisely demonstrates his purchasing power. During a visit with Edward Thomas, a fellow tourist, to see the 'Furietti Centaurs', two famous black marble statues found sometime earlier in Hadrian's Villa at Tivoli, Leeson decided to make an offer of £2,000 for them which regrettably for him was immediately rejected with indignation.[14] From an important source, we know that in the same period he was also planning to go to Naples and that he acquired the assistance of the young scholar Robert Wood.[15] In March he commissioned a copy of a well known picture by Salvator Rosa from Joseph Vernet (no. 41). In the same month came the news that a merchant ship carrying a cargo said to be worth £60,000 including statues and pictures belonging to Leeson was captured by a French privateer.[16] Unfortunately we do not know what works of art were contained in that boat and so we cannot judge the wisdom of Leeson's purchases. We may presume that his choice would have been influenced by the *virtù* of his Roman acquaintances.

Fig. 1 The facade of Russborough

In the years following his return to Ireland he was occupied with Russborough which must have been completed only around 1748, but in his mind he was planning one more trip to Italy.[17] This time he was accompanied by his elder son Joseph and his nephew Joseph Henry, his sister Anne's son. Before the end of March 1750, he was probably already settled in Rome. The number of foreign visitors had noticeably increased in the city and Leeson with the two young men became a significant part of the British and Irish community which revolved around the 'Spanish Steps', in the area the local inhabitants called *'il Ghetto degli Inglesi'*. Among the fellow tourists they met were some Irish acquaintances, like Lord Charlemont and Thomas Dawson (figs. 13 and 20) and several young British artists who were busily engaged with the double task of improving their skill by sketching monuments and works of art and with their constant attempts to obtain new commissions from their wealthy compatriots.

Undoubtedly there was a lot of imitation among the tourists regarding what should be acquired, and from which artist, sometimes leading to harsh competition among the latter, but the quality and taste of Pompeo Batoni's portraits were beyond any challenge and Leeson appealed to him once again for a number of these representing his closest relatives (nos. 8, 11 and 12). Joshua Reynolds, not yet famous, was in Rome at the same time and from him instead Leeson commissioned some caricatures, the success of which induced the painter to execute a few more for other 'gentlemen friends'.[18]

The young Joseph Henry, who must have been keen in classical studies before he went to Italy, gained a reputation as something of an expert in antiquities.[19] He commissioned the most complex of Reynolds' caricatures, *The Parody of Raphael's 'School of Athens'* (no. 19), as well as two landscapes of Tivoli from Richard Wilson (fig. 2).[20] As we now know, he left Rome for

*Fig. 2 Richard Wilson,
View from Tivoli over the Campagna, 1752,
National Gallery of Ireland*

Venice on 12 May 1751, but it is not clear whether in the company of his relatives or not.[21] His Grand Tour extended to France and Spain and took many years.[22] From this and other trips to Italy he brought back paintings by Batoni, Vernet, Martin, Dolci, Joli and Mannozzi.[23]

Henry's uncle Joseph Leeson had perhaps already returned to Ireland before the end of 1751 since in the following spring it was reported that he was about to act with 'some ladies and gentlemen', in Rowe's *The Fair Penitent*.[24] Some works of art brought this time from Italy, or sent later to him, are identifiable. There were four oval landscapes by Joseph Vernet (nos. 33-36) and two pairs of marble sculptures after Graeco-Roman pieces, one made in Rome by Bartolomeo Cavaceppi (nos. 46 and 47), and one in Florence after the celebrated statues in the Uffizi Tribuna by Giovanni Battista Piamontini (nos. 42 and 43). From Florence came a scagliola table-top crafted by a monk named Pietro Belloni (fig. 3 and no. 24), and probably the bulk of the seventeenth-century painted canvases of their collection.[25]

Unfortunately, it seems that none of the Leesons kept a travelling journal or account book, nor has any of their correspondence from that time ever been found. It is nonetheless clear that Joseph Leeson's artistic patronage did not rest solely with his Grand Tour purchases: once back in Ireland he found his palatial residence of Russborough complete.[26] The house must have looked superb, as it still does today, constructed in granite, with the main block flanked by two curved colonnades, filled with classical statues, and forming an elegant semicircular space at the front of the building (fig. 1). The inside was no less important with plaster-work decoration of

Fig. 3 Detail of no. 24 showing signature of Pietro Belloni

the richest late Baroque, almost certainly commissioned from the Ticinesi brothers Lafranchini (fig. 4), and the walls covered with landscapes by George Barret, tastefully framed with stucco. The surrounding setting of the house was then quite different from how it looks now. The beech trees which were planted by the Leesons must have taken some time before maturing into the present rows and woodland. Before the construction of the dam to create the Poulaphouca reservoir in 1938, the Liffey river flowed with a waterfall (called the Poulaphouca Falls) along the lower part of the estate and nearby were artificial grottoes made by the first owners possibly in imitation of an Italian garden.[27]

In 1754 Leeson was elected a member of the Society of Dilettanti, and two years later he was made Baron of Russborough, probably to the surprise of few of his acquaintances.[28] He was one of the wealthiest men in Ireland and in spite of some of the excesses of his nature he and his family were largely accepted by the aristocracy and landed gentry. After four more years he was made Viscount and finally, in 1763, Earl of Milltown.[29]

His son Joseph, now Viscount Russborough, who appears to have been good-humoured but not particularly bright, was in the meantime pursuing the lifestyle of a fun-loving bachelor of disreputable character.[30]

In 1768, two years after his second wife's death, the Earl of Milltown married again. His new wife was Elizabeth French, daughter of the Very Reverend William French, Dean of Armagh. This third marriage did not pass without comment,[31] but whatever popular rumours were spread they did not impede the bestowal of a new personal honour on the 1st Earl and in 1770 he was made a member of the Privy Council for Ireland. Although over sixty years old, Lord Milltown seems to have been more active then ever and in 1776 he moved with his new young family into a new house which he had built on the more fashionable north side of the Green. There he lived for seven more years and, on 22 October 1783, he passed away.[32]

Joseph, the 2nd Earl, does not appear to have changed his lifestyle after his father's death. As the principal heir, he became the legitimate owner of

Fig. 4 Detail of plaster-work decoration on the staircase, Russborough

Russborough and, when in town, he lived in the old family residence left by the 1st Earl in 1776. With no ambition for politics, save for a brief involvement many years before,[33] he preferred to travel frequently abroad.[34] During those trips he certainly purchased more works of art and although we do not have any proof we can speculate that perhaps some of the French paintings in the collection were acquired by him.[35]

With the end of the century approaching, other Leesons went on their Grand Tour, but were remembered only for their youthful intemperance.[36] At the time of the 1798 insurrection, Russborough was occupied but left uninjured by the insurgents. By contrast many parts of the house were damaged by the behaviour of the royal troops who took control of the mansion immediately after, and sections of the roof were pulled down and used for firewood.[37] During this Vandalic episode the 2nd Earl was abroad once again and, just a little later, he ended his life at Chelsea in London, in 1801, and was buried in St James' Church, Westminster.[38]

His brother Brice became the 3rd Earl and on him fell the burden of the restoration of Russborough.[39] All through the nineteenth century successive Earls added further *objets d'art* to the already famous family collection but, regrettably, no one was gifted with the same *virtù* or the same wealth as the 1st Lord Milltown.

With the extinction of the direct male line, in 1899 Lady Geraldine, Dowager Countess of Milltown, definitively decided to donate almost the entire contents of Russborough to the National Gallery of Ireland. The complicated bequest was finalised in 1902 and since then millions of visitors have enjoyed and admired the beauty and the variety of the collection. Meanwhile, the mansion followed a different fortune, and was acquired in 1952 by Sir Alfred and Lady Beit and through their enlightened patronage it was restored to its pristine splendour.

* This epigram was coined by Laetitia Pilkington in 1748-49 when rumours of a possible elevation of Joseph Leeson Senior to a baronetcy were spreading in Irish society: see Pilkington 1754, vol. 2 [1997 ed.] p.691.
1. Burke's Peerage, p.1827.
2. 'Fanatic brewer, reported to have some hundreds of houses in this town' from Swift Maxims, *ca.*1728, vol. 12, p.135.
3. Georgian Society Records [GSR], vol. II, 1910, pp.32-33.
4. *Ibidem*, p.91.
5. The Register of the Parish of St Peter & St Kevin Church, 1669-1761. Parish Register Society of Dublin, 1911.
6. Burke's Peerage gives 1701; The Gentleman's Magazine at the date of his death in 1783 spoke of him in his 74th year (i.e. born in 1709); The Complete Peerage said he was born on 11 March 1711.
7. Pilkington 1754, vol. 1 [1997 ed.], p.303.
8. Anne Preston was the niece of the exchequer judge Arthur Dawson who owned two lots on the north side of St Stephen's Green, beside those of the Leesons.
9. The Gentleman's Magazine, 1783.
10. GSR, vol. V, 1913, p.68.
11. To Patrick Sweetman: see GSR, vol. II, 1910, p.88.
12. The Complete Peerage, p.708.
13. Laetitia Pilkington referred to a scandalous episode which occurred one night in a house in Glasnevin involving Leeson with a young girl, her widow mother and Leeson's father. See Pilkington 1754, vol. I, p.303.
14. Edward Thomas in a letter to Dr Jeremiah Milles, dated Rome, 6 January 1751, British Museum, Add, MS. 19,941, f.33. On the 'Furietti Centaurs' see Haskell and Penny 1981, pp.178-79.
15. Letter from Cardinal Albani to Sir Horace Mann, Rome 15 January 1745, PRO London, State Papers, Ms. 98/50, f.35 v.; letter from Sir Horace Mann to the Duke of Newcastle, Florence 26 January 1744, PRO London, State Papers, Ms. 98/50, f.33 r..
16. Walpole Correspondance, vol. IXX, p.13, n.26.
17. 'A noble new house forming into perfection', A Tour of Two Gentlemen 1748, p.243.
18. Reynolds painted three caricatures for Joseph Leeson (see nos. 20-22), one for William Lowther (no. 23), one for John Woodyeare (fig. 23) and the *Parody* for his nephew Joseph Henry (no. 19). Later he painted a burlesque episode on a journey for Ralph Howard of Shelton Abbey, Co. Wicklow.
19. 'Is Jo: Henry at Rome now? Is he as fine a gentleman as ever ...or is he more affected since he has trod on classic ground, seen every court, heard every king declare his royal sense of Operas and the fair': this long sentence was included by Bishop Richard Marlay in a letter sent to Lord Charlemont in Rome, see Charlemont Manuscripts, 12.r. 21, no.101. See also C. O'Connor in Ingamells 1997, p.484. Pier Leone Ghezzi twice described Henry in his drawings as '... *Huomo assai erudito nelle antichitá* ...' (see no. 9, note 3).
20. The landscapes of Richard Wilson are also in the National Gallery of Ireland [NGI], inv. nos. 746 and 747.
21. This important reference was written by Pier Leone Ghezzi at the bottom of a pen drawing portrait of Henry, previously unpublished: '*partito da Roma per Venetia li 12 Maggio 1751*' (FN 4739, Rome, Istituto per la Grafica). The reason for his trip to Venice was certainly to attend the Ascension Feast-day, which in 1751 fell on 20 May.
22. Letter from J. Tyrrell to R. Howard, 8 October 1752, Wicklow Papers, National Library of Ireland [NLI].
23. Twiss 1777, pp.26-27.

24 'The Fair Penitent is to be acted in town by some ladies and gentlemen. Leeson is to play Lothario. They say he will do it very ill ...', 16 April 1752, letter from Bishop R. Marlay to Lord Charlemont, see Charlemont Manuscripts, p. 184. *The Fair Penitent* was written in 1703 by Nicholas Rowe (1674-1718), and 'Lothario' was the libertine character of that popular play.

25 See Wynne 1986.

26 In 1752 Bishop Pocock calls it a 'new built house', GSR, vol. V, 1913, Dublin, p.68.

27 'I told you I was to see Russborough; the house is really fine and furniture magnificent, but a frightful place; Mr. Leeson [probably Joseph Junior] carry'd us to see a very fine waterfall near it', from a letter of Emily Countess of Kildare to James Earl of Kildare, 9 May 1759, in Leinster Letters, vol. I, pp.76-77.

28 See Cust 1914, p. 258.

29 The Complete Peerage, p.708.

30 Sir Herbert Croft, in his satirical poem, 'The Abbey Kirklington Revived' (1780), described Lord Russborough as 'an incorrigible simpleton'. Mrs. Margaret Leeson, alias Peg Plunkett, a successful Dublin prostitute, by chance with an homonymous name, described Lord Russborough in Leeson Memoirs, p.107, as a 'constant visitor', who once showed his generosity and bought on her request 'the most elegant palliass I had ever seen, made quite in the French taste ... and [I] slept very comfortably on it that night, and indeed ever since ... and whilst I live I shall ever have a remembrance of Lord M----, about me '. And further on (pp.199-200), 'One evening as Joe the game cock and I, were talking ... a loud rap announced some person of consequence; when seeming terribly alarmed, lest it might be Buck Lawless with whom I lived at that time, I requested with tears in my eyes, his lordship would be kind enough to step into a clothes-press which stood in my dressing room, and on his lordship politely complying, I turned the key on him, and amused myself with my favourite L—g for about an hour, when I walked out with him, leaving his lordship a close prisoner till my return, when I had the honour of liberating him, almost stifled and pressed to death in the presence of eight or ten of my laughter-loving wenches, who absolutely were convulsed with laughing, at the ridiculous figure his lordship cut on being released from doing Cupboard duty'. The cover of the 1995 edition erroneously shows the portrait of *A Lady Leeson* by P. Batoni [NGI inv. no. 703], who obviously had nothing to do with the authoress of the memoirs.

31 The *Dublin Magazine*, on that occasion (1768), published the following rhyme:
Milltown coeval with thy sire
Did to a fair young maid aspire,
And felt or feigned a lover's fire
At seventy years or more.

32 The Complete Peerage 1932, p.708.

33 MP for Thomastown, 1757-60, *Ibidem*, p.709.

34 He appears to have travelled in France and Switzerland in 1770-71 and later almost continuously in Germany, Italy and France between 1777 and 1779: see no. 8.

35 See F. Croke in National Gallery of Ireland 1992, p.96. That he took pride in his collection is evident from the words of Topham Bowden 1791, p.70, 'Such is the urbanity of Lord Milltown that he takes pleasure in showing his house and paintings himself to all who have a curiosity to see them'. I am grateful to Chris Caffrey for this reference.

36 PRO, London, 30/9/43, Journal of Sarah Bentham, Rome 23 February 1794: 'A disturbance at the opera produced by Mr Brand's appearing in "Dirty dress" with cropped hair. Mr Brand was at this time travelling with Mr Leeson an Irish Gentleman brother to Lord Milltown; both Thouthless and dissipated and both declaring they would go together in future to every Roman conversatione in the same kind of dress but they were soon given to understand how much such an apperance would displease Every Englishman as well as the Romans'.

37 GSR, 1913, p.69.

38 The Complete Peerage 1932, p.709.

39 GSR, *loc. cit*.

An episode in the life of the 2nd Earl of Milltown

The following letter was written by Thomas P. Butler and sent from Castlebar, Co. Mayo, to William Lee of the 16th Dragoon Guards at Thetford, Norfolk.

April 22nd 1792

My dear Lee,

FitzGerald is very uneasy at not hearing whether his reply to Morgan's adress to the public has been inserted, least his supposed silence should condemn him : pray let me know as soon as you can possibly whether it has appeared in the paper or not - I set off this letter at random to you at Thetford, for it's not unlikely but that you may be gone to headquarters to prepare for the Review, but at apropos: I am surprised Harcourt has not joined yet, I suppose he's not out of dock[1] yet. I heard he got a devil of shot between wind and water[2] from a London frigate,[3] in short he kept his Christmas as merrily as yourself. There is a club in Dublin lately establish'd that would be the very thing for him - Your friend Lord Miltown is the author of it. It's called the Cherokee Club. There was a set of young fellows dined with him one day and insisted on dining in the best room; & set about chucking the wine upon his very fine carpet; & in short did all the mischief they could - the old bumbrusher the next day was making a heavy complint about this, & said that a set of Cherokees couldn't have served him worse : they heard this, formed a club & enrolled his Lordship as honorary member. The uniform is black turned up with red.

It's a long time since I toss'd you any slang : take a little now - I'll be up to they in your pipes & toss you your guts for garters.

This requires a note of explanation. There is a cutler of great repute in Dublin of the name Lamprey & his name is on his knives. I'll leave you to make out the rest.

I must now have done, for the man waits to take this to the post,

believe Dr Lee, Most sincerely
Yours, Thos. P. Butler

The letter was found by Mr Albert Mac Duff in 1990 and published in the Summer 1991 issue of the magazine *Irish Stamps News*.

1   *dock* = hospital.
2   *shot between wind and water* = infected with venereal disease.
3   *frigate* = prostitute.

Detail of Joseph Henry of Straffan (1727-1796) *by Pompeo Batoni, no. 9*

the **Portraits**

ANONYMOUS

1 *Joseph Leeson of St Stephen's Green (1660-1741)*

Oil on panel, 37.7 x 31.8 cm

Inscribed: *Josephus Leeson/ Depictus 1718/ Eta ..s 56*

National Gallery of Ireland (inv. no. 1648)

2 *Margaret Leeson*

Oil on panel, 37.5 x 31.8 cm

Inscribed: Marg :[ta] *Leeson depic:* [a] */ anno 1718 AEtatis 36*

National Gallery of Ireland (inv. no. 1649)

Provenance: Earls of Milltown (nos. 110, 107, Deed of Gift)

Joseph and Margaret Leeson were married in 1695[1] and lived in 82, South St Stephen's Green.[2] She was the daughter and co-heir of Andrew Brice, Alderman and sometime Sheriff of Dublin,[3] and she gave birth to an uncertain number of children only four of whom survived to marry. Joseph, father of the 1st Earl, to whom he left his fortune, was a shrewd real estate speculator[4] and long time owner of a brewery which was kept at the rear of his house.[5]

In spite of the date of 1718 which is inscribed on both these portraits, there are some evident stylistic discrepancies which make them appear to have been painted much later during the century. Joseph Leeson's image in fact closely recalls that painted for his son by Batoni (no. 8). Not only is the pose of the sitter similar, with the left hand grabbing the gown along his waist, but so too is the use of a curtain in the background.

The pendant portrait of his wife Margaret Leeson also shows some inconsistencies with its inscribed date. The woman is represented wearing a rich vandykian dress with a large lace collar, quite premature to the fancy vogue which became popular in portraiture only a few decades later.

Although we cannot exclude the possibility that at least Joseph Leeson's portrait may recall an earlier picture of the same sitter, unfortunately unknown to us, we should consider Batoni's portrait of his son, dated 1744, as the only proper *terminus ante quem* for the execution of these portraits which we are tempted to dated late in the 1770s.

1 Burke's Peerage.
2 GSR, vol. II, 1910, pp.88-89. The house no longer exists.
3 Burke's Peerage.
4 Swift Maxims, vol. XII, p.135.
5 GSR, *op.cit.*, p.88.

1

2

ANTHONY LEE (fl.1724-1767)

3 *Joseph Leeson* later *1st Earl of Milltown (1711?-1783)*

Oil on canvas, 54 x 35.5 cm (relined, reduced on the lower edge)
Inscribed on the back of the frame: *Earl of Milltown to be sent on my death to my Nephews Richard John Leeson & Ralph Leeson of 5 Rosemount/Terrace North Circular Road Dublin- Florence de Marylska.*

Sir Roy Strong Collection

Provenance: by descent to Countess Florence Georgina Ostoja-Marylski; purchased on the London art market by Sir Roy Strong

The sitter was the first son of Joseph and Margaret Leeson and their legitimate heir.[1] We do not know about his education but we must presume that in keeping with the aspirations and ambitions of his father, it would have been the best that could be provided at the time to a 'gentleman'. Socially, he soon acquired the fame of an incorrigible libertine, a vice which he appears to have inherited from his father and which he transmitted to his elder son.[2]

Here the young and tall Joseph[3] is standing beside an arch while in the background two servants are holding the master's horse near the gate, ready for the ride. The scene fortunately bears some resemblance to a prospect of St Stephen's Green published in 1728, with the wall and the row of elm trees, which allows us to identify it as the outskirts of the Leeson's town house on the south side of the Green.[4]

This portrait is in my opinion the earliest of the two known to have been painted by Anthony Lee for Joseph Leeson, preceding the other, dated 1735 (no. 4), by only a few years. The man was still in his early twenties here, wearing long riding boots and holding his gloves under his arm, while his left hand is resting in the middle of his red jacket, following a well known habit of the time.

1 Lodge 1789, vol.3, p.125.
2 Pilkington 1754, vol. 1, pp.302, vol. 2, pp.691-92; Leinster Letters, vol. I, pp.76-77.
3 According to Mrs. Pilkington, Joseph Leeson was six foot high: Pilkington 1754, vol. I, p.302.
4 The 'Prospect' is in the margin of Brooking's Map of Dublin: see GSR, vol. II, 1910, p.36.

Essential Literature: Crookshank and The Knight of Glin 1978, p. 41, fig. 23.

ANTHONY LEE (fl.1724-1767)

4 *Joseph Leeson* later *1st Earl of Milltown (1711?-1783)*

Oil on canvas, 197.5 x 123.5 cm (reduced about 10 cm along the edges)

Signature lower left: *ALee Pinx / 1735*

National Gallery of Ireland (inv. no. 698)

Provenance: Earls of Milltown (no. 97, Deed of Gift)

At the time this picture was painted, Joseph Leeson had already been married for six years and was the father of two sons.[1] Anthony Lee was once again entrusted with the work: after all, he must have known the Leesons quite well and perhaps was even a close friend of the family since he too was living in South St Stephen's Green, only two houses away from them.[2]

The artist in this period was probably at the apex of his career and, as this picture shows, he was capable of producing portraits of quality without affectation. Leeson here is in his recurrent strutting pose with his left hand resting inside his jacket and wearing a very elegant frock-coat with knee-breeches and silk stockings, while his right hand is holding a three-cornered-style hat.

The architectural setting behind him, as has been suggested, could indicate his real interest in fashionable architecture of his day.[3] As is evident from the canvas' edges, originally the picture should have been wider by at least ten centimetres each side.[4]

The time around the middle of the eighteenth century was a period of transition for many Irish portraitists. Even for those most successful, their style was permanently characterised by the strong influences of Jervas or Hogarth. Among the painters in Ireland, Lee appears to have been closest to Stephen Slaughter[5] with whom he shared the same fondness for representing figures with rich and elaborate dress. In his later works the artist shows unfortunate signs of fatigue and his portraits are generally more stiff and naïve and lacking in liveliness.[6]

1 Burke's Peerage.
2 GSR, vol. II, 1910, p.89.
3 H. Potterton in Harbison et al. 1978, p.150.
4 From a list of works of art, hand-written at the end of nineteenth century, by Lady Geraldine Evelyn Leeson Countess of Milltown (NGI Archive), we know that this portrait hung in the Entrance Hall of Russborough House.
5 Crookshank and Knight of Glin 1969, p.39, n.28: the measurements given in that entry are inaccurate.
6 I refer in particular to the 1745 Brabazon portraits (private collection, Ireland).

Essential Literature: Strickland 1913, vol. II, p.16; Crookshank and Knight of Glin 1969, p.39, n.28; Wynne 1974, p.104; Potterton in Harbison et al. 1978, p.150, fig.151; Crookshank and Knight of Glin 1978, p.41; National Gallery of Ireland, 1981, *ad vocem*.

ANTHONY LEE (fl.1724-1767)

5 Cecilia Leeson née Leigh (died 1737)

Oil on canvas, 76.5 x 63 cm

National Gallery of Ireland (inv. no. 699)

Provenance: Earls of Milltown (no. 104, Deed of Gift)

6 A Lady Leeson

Oil on canvas, 76 x 63.5 cm

Sir Roy Strong Collection

Provenance: by descent to Countess Florence Georgina Ostoja-Marylski; purchased on the London art market by Sir Roy Strong

Cecilia was the first daughter of Francis Leigh, a landowner of Rathangan, Co. Kildare. On 20 January 1729 she married Joseph Leeson (1711?-1783).[1] She gave birth to three children and suddenly died young only a few years later allegedly from a disease contracted from her husband.[2]

We do not know who the lady in the second portrait is, and we can only speculate that it could be one of Joseph Leeson's sisters. The portrait of Cecilia carried the traditional attribution to Anthony Lee. There is no particular reason to doubt this authorship and it is evident that both portraits are by the same hand.

Since Cecilia Leeson died in 1737, her portrait could have been painted just a few years earlier, perhaps about 1735. At that time, there were at least five Leeson sisters alive, but two were already married. Of the remaining three, regrettably we know only their names, Martha, Mary and Margaret, and in theory, any one of these could be the lady portrayed in the second picture.

1 The Complete Peerage, p.708.
2 Pilkington 1754, vol. 1, pp.302-03, vol. 2, pp.691-92.
3 From a list of works of art, hand-written at the end of the nineteenth century by Lady Geraldine Evelyn Leeson Countess of Milltown (NGI Archive), we know that this portrait hung in the Boudoir of Russborough.

5

6

POMPEO BATONI (1708-1787)

7 *Joseph Leeson* later *1st Earl of Milltown, 1744*

Oil on canvas, 135.5 x 98.5 cm

Signed on the base of the column: *Pompeo Batoni. Pinse. Roma. 1744*

National Gallery of Ireland (inv. no. 701)

Provenance: Earls of Milltown (no. 435, Deed of Gift)

After the death of his first wife, Joseph Leeson, in 1738, got married again to Anne Preston of Swainstown, Co. Meath, and very soon, when his father passed away in 1741, he inherited enormous wealth[1] which allowed him to purchase a large property in County Wicklow, including the townland of Russellstown with its sub-denomination of Russellsborough where he planned to build his country residence.[2] The construction took many years and in the meantime Joseph, in accordance with the custom of any 'real gentleman', decided to depart for his Grand Tour through Europe. From two different sources of early 1745, we have proof that Joseph had arrived in Italy at least in 1744 and that he had visited Florence although he spent most of his time in Rome.[3] Consequently, this portrait, dated 1744, is the first record of his presence in Italy. The choice of the artist is very much in tune with Joseph Leeson's attitude, which appears to have always been to acquire what was reputed to be best. How Leeson came to know Batoni is not known but it is possible that it happened through a fellow traveller, Dr John Clephane.[4] At the time the painter was known primarily for his history pictures and he only later became acclaimed by British and Irish visitors as the best portraitist in Rome. We must, therefore, give credit to Leeson for having been one of the first, if not the very first, to choose to sit for him.[5]

Today, looking at this portrait, one aspect is immediately striking: the complete informality of the sitter simply wearing a domestic gown, a green silk fur-lined *robe de chambre*, with his matching fur hat. Although in wintertime the lack of efficient heating in Roman houses was notorious,[6] what the artist really wanted to represent was a portrait of a gentleman with a fully relaxed appearance, a quality which he applied to the majority of his subsequent portraits.[7] At the same time, Batoni succeeds in revealing some of Leeson's better known characteristics not least his pretentiousness and his vanity.

1. The Gentleman's Magazine, Dublin 1741.
2. GSR, vol. V, 1913, p.68.
3. '*Monsieur Lissoen Gentilhmme Anglois, qui depuis longtems est à Rome ...*', letter from Cardinal Albani to Sir Horace Mann, Rome 15 January 1745, PRO London, State Papers, Ms. 98/50, f.35v.; Walpole Correspondance, vol. IXX, p.13, n.26.
4. Clephane knew and corresponded with Batoni in 1741-42 and met Leeson in Rome in October 1744: see Ingamells 1997, p.215.
5. The Joseph Leeson portrait is the earliest exant example of a Grand Tourist painted by Batoni, but according to GSR, *op. cit.*, p.56, there was a previous one of Arthur Rowley, reputedly dated 1740 and lost in the fire of Summerhill House, Co. Meath, in 1922.
6. Francis Drake 'Account of a tour in Italy 1750-52', Magd. Oxford, MSS 246, 247; for a briefing see Ingamells 1997, p.310.
7. The portrait was mentioned hanging in the Small Dining Room in Russborough House by Neale 1826 and confirmed in the same location in a list, hand-written at the end of the nineteenth century by Lady Geraldine Evelyn Leeson Countess of Milltown (NGI Archive).

Essential Literature: Wynne 1974, p.104, fig.2; Bowron 1982, pp.9-10, 27-28; Clark 1985, pp.233-34, fig.86; Wynne 1986, pp.5-6, fig.7

POMPEO BATONI (1708-1787)

8 *Joseph Leeson* later **2nd Earl of Milltown (1730-1801)**

Oil on canvas, 99 x 73.5 cm

Signed on the base of the pilaster: *P.B. 1751*

National Gallery of Ireland (inv. no. 702)

Provenance: Earls of Milltown (no. 196, Deed of Gift)

Joseph Junior was the eldest son of Joseph Leeson, born from his first wife Cecilia Leigh. He was sent to Eton when he was twelve. Later, in 1750, with his cousin Joseph Henry of Straffan, he accompanied his father on his second Grand Tour. It is not clear if they arrived in Rome together because in the census of the inhabitants of the city carried through the Parish districts just before Easter of that year,[1] the only member of the family mentioned is Joseph, the elder, living near 'Piazza di Spagna'.[2] Before arriving in Rome it is likely that the young Leeson spent some time in Turin where he frequented the Royal Academy.[3] There he made an acquaintance who was revealed many years later by another young noble Irish traveller.[4] The first record of him in Rome is a Ghezzi pen drawing dated 27 October 1750 (fig. 7).[5] Instead this Batoni, judging from the sitter's gown, must have been carried out in the early months of 1751 since it is more than possible that at the end of the same year the Leesons were already on their way back to Ireland.[6]

The composition is very similar to the one made six years earlier for his father, with the difference that here the young man is facing the opposite way. The canvas, which is smaller than the previous one, appears to have been the size favoured by the artist for his half-figure portraits of that period. In spite of the indubitable unattractiveness of the sitter, Batoni was as usual able to render an image of refined elegance with great artifice.

During his life Joseph Leeson Junior made at least one more trip to Italy in 1778 as Lord Russborough, which is documented by different sources.[7] At the time of the 1798 Insurrection in Ireland, it seems he was in Italy, in which case it was his last trip there, since he died just three years later.[8]

1 In 1750 Easter was on 11 April.
2 '*Monsiu Lisson, Monsu Arvi, tre servi*', AVR Stati delle Anime, San Lorenzo in Lucina. We do not know who the '*Monsu Arvi*' sharing the house with Leeson could be. The suggestion that he might be Joseph Henry (Wynne 1974, p.106) is not convincing. It is phonetically more probable to be a Mr 'Harvey' or 'Hervey'. My suggestion is that it could be Captain Augustus J. Hervey. He is documented in Italy in 1747-48 and again between 1752 and 1758: see Ingamells 1997, p.488. He must have been in Italy also in 1750-51 because in the *Antichità Siciliane*, published by Giuseppe Maria Pancrazi in Naples (1751-52), one of the plates is dedicated to him. Among the other dedications there is one also to Joseph Henry.
3 Michael Wynne suggested instead that young Leeson was left 'by his father on his way home'. If so, it should be at the end of 1751 or at the beginning of 1752: see Wynne 1996[1], p.150. Unfortunately, we do not know precisely in which year Joseph Leeson Junior stayed in Turin because the records of the local Academy are are lost (information kindly provided by M. Wynne).
4 Leinster Letters, 259, Letter of William, Marquis of Kildare to Emily Duchess of Leinster, Turin 22 June 1768, vol. III, p.525. See p.33, note 6.
5 Istituto Nazionale per la Grafica, Rome (FN 19843), inscribed at the bottom: *Monsieur Lisson Inglese fatto da Mè Cav.' Ghezzi 27 8bre - 1750 -*.
6 Letter of R. Marlay to Lord Charlemont, see Charlemont Manuscripts, p.184.
7 Letters of J. Collet to W.D. Poyntz, 28 March and 3 October 1778, Genoese Consular Correspondence 1776-79, MSS; *Gazzetta Toscana*, Florence, 8 August 1778, XIII, p.127.

8 GSR, vol. V, 1913, p.69. Neale 1826 mentions the portrait hanging in the first room in Russborough. And it is recorded in the Small Drawing Room in a list, hand-written at the end of the nineteenth century, by Lady Geraldine Evelyn Leeson Countess of Milltown (NGI Archive)

Essential Literature: Neale 1826; Clark 1985, p.250, fig.138; Wynne 1986, pp.6-7, fig.8.

POMPEO BATONI (1708-1787)

9 *Joseph Henry of Straffan (1727-1796)*

Oil on canvas, 98 x 72.5 cm

The Walters Art Gallery, Baltimore (37. 1932)

Provenance: Don Marcello Massarenti, Rome; Henry Walters, Baltimore 1902; bequeathed by Walters to the city of Baltimore in 1931

The sitter was the son of Hugh Henry, a merchant and Dublin banker, and of Anne Leeson, sister of Joseph, 1st Earl of Milltown. In 1743 he inherited the large estate of Straffan in Co. Kildare.[1] The first information about his Grand Tour came from a letter written from Dublin by the wit Richard Marlay to Lord Charlemont where he briefly mentions some qualities which were later frequently associated with Henry.[2] Whatever date we presume for his arrival in Rome he was certainly there in the late months of 1750 when he was portrayed in several drawings by Pier Leone Ghezzi.[3] In 1751, he was also included in two of Reynolds' caricatures, the larger of which, the *Parody of the 'School of Athens'* (no. 19) was personally commissioned by him from the artist. On the basis of those pictures Anthony Clark was able to identify the present portrait.

The pose assumed here by Henry, holding a small book and resting one arm on a pedestal, is recurrent in Batoni's portraits and serves to create a feeling of calm and contemplation. His clothes show no ostentation. The elegant and sober frock-coat with a turned down buff collar is made of velvet, while from his waistcoat emerges a fine gauze shirt. His bright red breeches, which according to the fashion of the period were fastened below the knee, are also worn by him in the two Reynolds caricatures referred to.[4]

It is almost certain that Henry owned another painting by Batoni which unfortunately seems to be lost.[5] During his stay in Rome he also ordered two landscapes from Richard Wilson[6] and later, four from Vernet.[7] Henry did not follow his Leeson relatives and instead returned to Ireland some time later. In 1752 he spent the summer in Marseilles[8] before proceeding to Spain, where he purchased several landscapes painted by Antonio Joli.[9]

In 1755 he was once again in Italy, and in Pisa he met Robert Adam who he happened to meet again in Florence two years later through Sir Horace Mann, the British representative to the Grand Duke of Tuscany.[10] In Florence (which he preferred to Rome on this trip) he purchased many more works of art. Finally in the early 1760s his peregrination ended[11] and in 1764 he married Lady Catherina Rawdon, daughter of the 1st Earl of Moira.[12]

1 Burke's Landed Gentry, p.311.
2 Charlemont Manuscripts, 12.r. 21, no.101; see also C. O'Connor in Ingamells 1997, p.484.
3 See fig. 9. The hand written inscription along the bottom by P.L. Ghezzi reads: *Monsiur Giuseppe Henry Inglese uomo assai erudito nelle antichità 9bre 1750* and added later by the same hand: *partito da Roma per Venetia li 12 Maggio 1751*; and fig. 8 inscribed: *Mon'. Henry fatto da Mè Ghezzi 27 Xbre 50*. Both drawings are in the Istituto Nazionale della Grafica, Rome (FN 4739 and FN 4738).
4 See nos. 15 and 21.
5 Twiss 1777, p.26.
6 Both were included in the 1902 Milltown Gift to the NGI, inv. nos. 746-747 (Deed of Gift nos. 184-185). See also p. 3.

9

7 Lagrange 1864, pp.336-37. See nos. 33-36.
8 Wicklow Papers, letter of J. Tyrrell to R. Howard, 8 October 1752, NLI.
9 Twiss 1777, *loc. cit.*; see also no. 44.
10 Fleming 1962, pp.128-29, 232-33.
11 Leinster Letters, vol. I, p.104.
12 Burke's Landed Gentry, p.311.

Essential Literature. Clark 1985, p.250, fig. 137.

Attributed to GAVIN HAMILTON (1723-1798)

10 *Robert Wood (1717?-1771)*

Oil on canvas, 58.9 x 50.5 cm

Private Collection

Provenance: by descent to the Chandler family, James Adam & Sons Dublin, 22 November 1990, lot 148, where bought by the present owner

Already travelling through Europe to Italy in his twenties, Robert Wood's lifelong intention was to pursue and recover the classical culture of ancient times. Born in Riverstown Castle to James Wood of Summerhill, Co. Meath, Robert studied first in Glasgow in 1738 after which he obtained a doctorate in Padua, the oldest university in Europe.[1] In May 1742 he sailed from Venice to the Ionian and Aegean Islands and reached Damietta in Egypt.[2] In Italy on his return, in 1744, he met Joseph Leeson and became his secretary [3] and probably his adviser for the purchase of works of art. Although the influence of Wood on Joseph Leeson's taste is largely a matter of speculation, we have proof that on at least one occasion he acted as agent for him.[4]

In May 1750, with John Bouverie, James Dawkins and the draughtsman Giovan Battista Borra, Wood set sail from Naples on his most famous expedition to the East. After a stop over in Athens where with his companions he met Stuart and Revett,[5] he finally reached the abandoned ancient cities of Palmyra and Baalbec, whose ruins were investigated in detail and published by him in two successive books.[6] In Italy once again in 1754, Robert Wood acted as 'bear-leader' to the young Duke of Bridgewater. During his sojourn in Rome he befriended Robert Adam[7] and Allan Ramsay. The latter painted a portrait of him in 1755 now in the National Portrait Gallery, London.[8] A second portrait was commissioned by the Duke of Bridgewater from Anton Raphael Mengs in the same year,[9] but the most celebrated image of Robert Wood is that with Dawkis arriving at Palmyra in 1751 which was painted on a large canvas by Gavin Hamilton (1757-1758).[10] The present portrait shows a strong similarity to the image painted by Hamilton and from its provenance it appears to have been owned by the traveller and antiquarian Richard Chandler who was a member of the Society of Dilettanti and a friend of Robert Wood.

1 Morpugo 1927, p.73: 15 July 1738, '*D. Robertus Wood, Hibernus, D. Alexandri filius, lauream in Philosophia et Medicina consecutus est*'.
2 DNB 1968, vol. XXI, p.844.
3 Letter from Cardinal Albani to Sir Horace Mann, Rome 15 January 1745, PRO London, State Papers, Ms. 98/50, f.35v.; letter from Sir Horace Mann to the Duke of Newcastle, Florence 26 January 1744, PRO London, State Papers, Ms. 98/50, f.33 r..
4 On 5 December 1749, Wood commissioned four oval landscapes from Joseph Vernet on behalf of Joseph Leeson: see nos. 33-36.
5 DNB *loc. cit.*.
6 Wood 1753 and 1757.
7 Fleming 1962, pp.148-49, 171, 176.
8 Fleming 1957, p.76.
9 Roëttgen 1993, p.19, fig. 8.
10 The canvas was commissioned by Henry Dawkins after the death of his brother James in December 1757. The painting is now in the Hunterian Museum in Glasgow.
11 The Gavin Hamilton attribution was made by David White who recovered this portrait and who will soon publish it. I am indebted to him for the information regarding the provenance. On a purely technical aspect, the picture is still in its original stretcher and frame. The quality and proportions of these indicate it is English, and the type of canvas is definitely not Italian.

10

POMPEO BATONI (1708-1787)

11 *A Lady of the Leeson Family as a Shepherdess*

Oil on canvas, 49.9 x 39.5 cm (painted surface 47.2 x 36.2 cm)

Signed on the rock: *P.B. 1751*

Sir Denis Mahon Collection

Provenance: Earls of Milltown (no. 301, Deed of Gift); Sotheby's London, 1 June 1960, lot 41; bought by Julius Weitzner from whom it was acquired by Sir Denis Mahon

12 *A Lady of the Leeson Family as Diana,* traditionally called **Anne Leeson,** later **1st Countess Milltown**

Oil on canvas, 50 x 39.5 cm (painted surface 47 x 36 cm)
Signed on the rock: *P.B. 1751*

National Gallery of Ireland (inv. no. 703)

Provenance: Earls of Milltown (no. 110, Deed of Gift)

There is no evidence that any female members of the Leeson family went to Italy in the eighteenth century. Therefore, as Anthony Clark first suggested, these two portraits must have been painted by Batoni using miniatures carried by some of the gentlemen.[1] Without some comparable contemporary portraits the identification of the two ladies is practically impossible. The more obvious claimants seem to be Anne Preston, second wife of the 1st Earl, and Mary, the only daughter from his first marriage. To complicate their recognition is the fact that both, in different measure, bear some resemblance to Joseph Leeson Junior. If this observation is correct, it would rule out the hypothesis that one of the portraits belongs to the Earl's second wife.

Equally, we cannot fully rely on the pictorial attributes of the two ladies. The representation of a woman as Diana does not refer automatically to her virginal quality, but could just recall her interest in some aspect of the natural life.[2] Similarly, the presence of a lamb could suggest meekness and submission but, on the other hand, there is evidence that the use of certain costumes in portraits was also dictated by the lasting fashion for mascherades.[3]

The earliest record of these two portraits is in Neale's 1826 description of the seat of Russborough.[4] In that list and in the same room another painting representing Juno is mentioned, but no author is given for it. In the hand-written inventory made by the Dowager Countess Geraldine at the end of the century three paintings are recorded, and this time all are said to be by Batoni.[5] In later records only the two portraits here exhibited are reported and particularly in 1902 they are both listed in the Deed of Gift, the legal act which officially sanctioned the bequest of the Milltown Collection to the National Gallery of Ireland.[6] How the two portraits became separated can only be speculated. The Milltown pictures reached the Gallery in 1906 when the new wing was finally constructed and in March of the same year, in the check list taken in Russborough before their transport to the Gallery, the two pictures were still included.[7]

11

1 The suggestion was made in a letter addressed to Denis Mahon.
2 In the same years Batoni painted other portraits of married ladies as Diana, e.g. *The Duchess of Sermoneta* and *Lady Fetherstonaugh*. Nevertheless, one more possibility which cannot be excluded is that this is Margaret Leeson, younger sister of the 1st Earl who died in 1742 and was portrayed with the help of a miniature.
3 Ribeiro 1995, p.183.
4 Neale 1826, 'Second Room: ... A Shepherdess — Pompeo Battoni ... A Juno ... Diana — Pompeo Battoni'
5 *Ibidem*, 'Music Room Pictures: P. Battoni - Portrait of a Lady as Diana & Sheperdess ... P. Battoni -Portrait of a Lady with a Peacock'.
6 Milltown Deed of Gift, NGI Archive: '110. Anne Countess of Milltown (1751) (17¾ in. H by 12½ in. W), 301. Peasant Girl (18½ in. H by 14½ in. W).
7 Milltowns papers, NGI Archive.

Essential Literature: Wynne 1974, p.106, fig.6; Clark 1985, pp.250-51, figs.139-40; Wynne 1986, pp.7- 8, figs.9-10; Finaldi 1997, p.30.

12

Attributed to ROBERT HUNTER (*fl*.1750-1803)

13 *Joseph Leeson as Lord Russborough, ca.1770*

Oil on canvas, 76.5 x 63.5 cm (original lining)

Private Collection

Provenance: by descent in the Clements family

This picture, which until recently was attributed to Arthur Devis, was traditionally said to have been given by Lord Russborough himself to Lady Elizabeth, wife of Robert Clements, 1st Earl of Leitrim, and this may indeed be true. The recently proposed author is Robert Hunter, an elusive artist born in Ulster with a career marked by the most manifest eclecticism.[1] If the date proposed for this canvas is correct, Lord Russborough would have been in his fifties. One more portrait of him, executed in pastel by Hugh Douglas Hamilton probably about the same time, was once documented in Carton House.[2]

The sitter is here portrayed standing outside by a classical vase on the steps of a country residence. His short cloak, decorated with loops, and the feathered hat show the man wearing a sort of costume used on occasion of a masquerade.[3] As we know, these episodes were a common occurrence in the *beau monde* of the Viscount, like participating with his friends and neighbours in staging plays or attending musical parties.[4] His social condition, his wealth and probably his total indifference to any aspect of public life allowed him to conduct a frivolous existence of non-events or small incidents reported by his closest acquaintances.[5] His frequent travels abroad were certainly a source of regular pleasure for him and became a constant habit in his more advanced age, and it was during his last absence from Ireland that he died in London in 1802.[6]

1 Strickland 1913, vol. I, pp.536-39; Crookshank 1989-90, pp.169-85.

2 Strickland 1913, vol. I, p.442.

3 Crookshank 1989-90, p.183, in attributing this picture to Robert Hunter, suggested that it could have been executed at the same time as a portrait of Thomas Connolly (private collection), signed and dated by Hunter in 1771. The two portraits share not only the same size but also a similar fancy costume which could lead one to suspect that they were painted for the same occasion.

4 Fitzgerald 1950, pp.94-95: one occasion of the kind was described in October 1775 in a letter to her sister the widow Duchess of Leinster by Lady Louisa Connolly. One evening in Castletown, Lord Russborough flirted openly with another guest, Mrs Macartney. The next day, after Leeson had left, Mrs Macartney amused the rest of the house guests with some verses that she had promptly written on the subject of Lord Russborough's passion for her. The company then decided, all dressed in fancy costumes, to reach Killadoon where they knew Rusborough was dining, hosted by Lady Elizabeth Clements, with William and Emily, Duke and Duchess of Leinster. After the initial surprise, they all enjoyed the scene which ended with Miss Lyttelton falling upon her knees and presenting the verses to Lord Russborough. The following evening back in Castletown Lady Louisa, seated in the Gallery, wrote to her sister about the events of the previous days, adding 'I believe I am writing a good deal of nonsense, for there is such a noise in the room I don't know what I am doing, and Lord Russborough is hurrying me to carry the letter to town.'

5 Fitzgerald 1949, pp.103-04: letter of Emily Marchioness of Kildare to James Marquess of Kildare, Carton, November 1762, 'I really believe Ld Kerry and Mr Leeson must fight in consequence of a violent quarrel they had t'other night at Mrs Martin's, on account of Mr Leeson's saying the Girouette (as he calls her), the new dancer, who it seems is frightfully ugly & old, was reckoned very like a lady in this town. He named no names, but a lady in company took it to herself (for whom to be sure he intended it), and say'd that if it was a woman that had found out such a likeness for her she shou'd forgive it, supposing that must proceed from envy (looking at Ld Kerry), but if it was a man she must tell him he was very impertinent and shou'd have every bone in his body broke. Many smart repartees follow'd between her and poor Dody; but at last Ld Kerry interfered, abused his family, etc; in short, sent him away in a violent passion, which luckily for me he came and vented here, telling Louisa and I the whole story in a very ridiculous way and mimicking the lady so well that it was delightful, But I now hear it will come to something serious; but I hope they will think better of it.'

6 He is documented to have travelled in France and Switzerland in 1770-71 and in Germany, Italy and France between 1777 and 1779. During these trips it appears that his personality provoked varying reactions from the people he met. At Lausanne on 17 July 1771 '...drunk tea with Ld Russborough

13

in a myrtle bower, laughed at his humor' was reported by Mrs Jane Home (SRO, Home of Wedderburn MSS, GD 267/ 33/ 1, Mrs Jane Graham Home Journal, 1771-72). In a letter adressed by William Marquess of Kildare to his mother the Duchess of Leinster from Turin 22 June 1768, he asks her to 'Pray tell Lord Russborough that Madame St. Gille says it is very hard he won't send her his picture' (Leinster Letters, vol. III, p.525). According to Michael Wynne, the real Madame St. Gille is the Contessa di San Gillio, and she could have been a fellow student of his in the Turin Royal Academy (see Wynne 1996[1], pp.150-51). In any case the woman must have been well acquainted with many Grand Tourists as may be inferred from a letter written by Lady Holland to her sister, the Marchioness of Kildare, from Turin, on 29 October 1766: 'I have seen Madame St. Gille, the famous Italian Lady all our men are so fond of. She don't strike me as so enchanting, I must confess' (Leinster Letters, vol. I, p. 476). When in October 1778, Lord Russborough was passing through Savona, John Collet the British Consul in Genoa in a letter to W.D. Poynty, British Chargé d'Affairs at Turin, reported: 'Lord Russborough was at Savona t'other day, I am very glad he miss'd Genoa and Turin....' (M. Wynne in Ingamells 1997, p.594).

Essential Literature: Strickland 1913, vol I, pp.536-39; Crookshank and Knight of Glin 1978, pp.83-86; Crookshank 1989-90, pp.169-85.

ANONYMOUS

14 *Joseph Earl of Milltown with his Family, ca.1772.*

Oil on canvas, 65 x 46.7 cm (painted surface 64 x 45 cm; canvas reduced on the left side)

National Gallery of Ireland (inv. no. 1697)

Provenance: by descent to Lord Cloncurry and by him bequeathed to the National Gallery of Ireland in 1928

In this family group the 1st Earl of Milltown is shown with his third wife Elizabeth, daughter of the Very Revd William French, Dean of Armagh. The Countess is holding her first daughter Cecilia, while the young boy offering a rose to the child is supposed to be Joseph, the son of Brice, the 3rd Earl.[1]

A painting with three figures, now lost but probably the prototype for this one, was included in the 1902 Milltown Gift.[2] That picture, like many others in the collection, carried the attribution to Batoni and a date of 1772. There is no record of a third trip to Rome by the 1st Earl at that time and it is difficult to imagine him, aged sixty, taking a long trip with his wife and a one-year-old child. Although it is possible that the group portrait could once again have been executed by Batoni using some miniatures brought to him by Lord Russborough, we prefer to think that the picture listed in 1902 was painted by a local artist and at some time 'upgraded' by having Batoni's name assigned to it.

If the group here exhibited, as we suspect, is a partial copy of that composition, we must imagine that the figure of the young boy was an addition while the figure of the 1st Earl was copied from the portrait by Batoni painted in 1744 (see no. 8).

In 1776, the 1st Earl with his young family moved to a newly built townhouse at no. 17, North St Stephen's Green, leaving the old one to his son Lord Russborough.[3] There Joseph Leeson, 1st Earl of Milltown died in 1783.[4] His widow remained in that house until 1795 when she sold it to William Newcome, Archbishop of Armagh and moved nearby to no. 11, Upper Merrion Street where she lived for the rest of her life until 1848.[5]

1. A paper label was found on the back of the canvas: *I bequeath this portrait to the National Gallery of Ireland as it was this Lord Russborough (afterwards Earl of Milltown) who formed the 'Milltown Collection' at the National Gallery. This portrait was painted in Rome 1757 by the celebrated Pompeo Battoni. Signed Hon: Fred.ᵇ Lawless.*
2. Milltown Deed of Gift, no.118, 'Portrait Group (Joseph, First Earl of Milltown, and Elizabeth, Countess of ditto, with Lady Cecilie Leeson, afterwards Latouche) 1772, 2 ft. 1½ in. H 1 ft. 7 in. W', Milltown papers, NGI Archive.
3. In 1776 the Earl already had four children by his third wife, the eldest was 6 years old.
4. GSR, vol. II, 1910, pp.47-48.
5. In 1811 Elizabeth, Dowager Countess Milltown, sold 88 paintings, largely eighteenth-century Irish landscapes, at auction at no. 16, Bean- Walk, St Stephen's Green. The only known copy of the sale catalogue is in The Barber Institute of Fine Arts, Birmingham University, Birmingham: I am obliged to Nicola Figgis for this information.

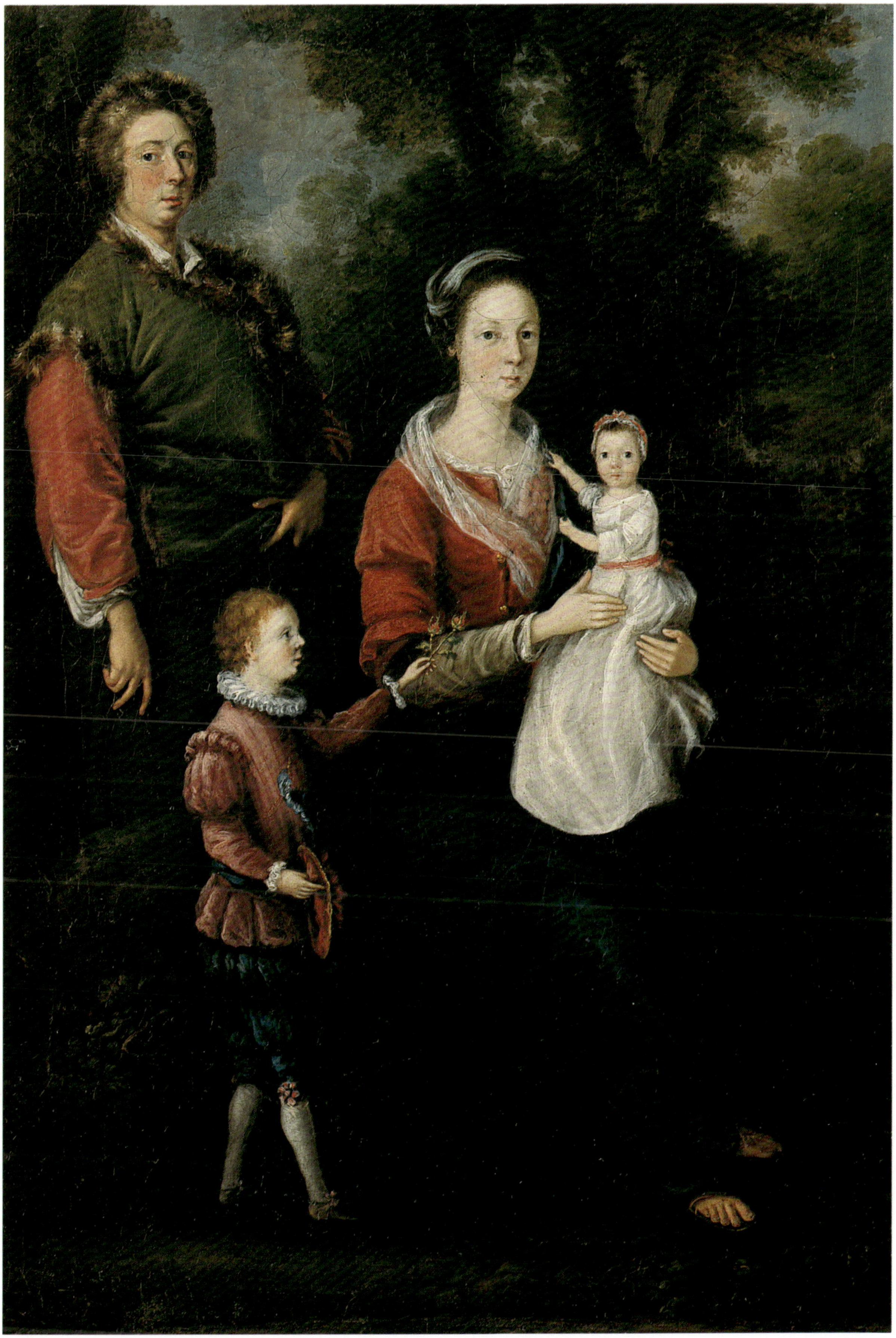

14

Fig. 5 Pier Leone Ghezzi, Joseph Henry, *pen and brown ink on paper, Metropolitan Museum of Art, New York (Rogers Fund, 1973)*

the Caricature

Sergio Benedetti

The representation of grotesque images in paintings, drawings and graffiti can be found since ancient times, from Egyptian tombs to Pompeiian walls. The word itself, originally meaning 'overloading' in the Italian language, was gradually adopted in the seventeenth century with the connotation of exaggerating the features of someone in a burlesque manner. Although this genre was practised before, it was only with Carracci, Guercino, Bernini and Callot that it assumed the aspect of a fully acceptable and accomplished artistic expression and a relieved distraction for the artist himself from the more demanding official employments.[1] The two rules which should be followed, whoever was the designated subject, were to accentuate and distort the character and physical defects of the unfortunate person, while at the same time carefully maintaining sufficient physiognomic traits to make him always identifiable to his community or to his circle of acquaintances and in such a way as to provoke their laughter and their mockery. In Venice, at the beginning of the eighteenth century, the daily stage of masked people during the Carnival and the *vis comica* of the *Commedia dell'Arte* offered innumerable models to feed the leisurely pens of Antonio Maria Zanetti the Elder, Gianbattista Tiepolo, and later of his son Giandomenico.

Further south, in Rome, the members of the local aristocracy, the antiquarians and the foreign visitors were instead the target of the caricatures produced by Pier Leone Ghezzi. The English painter Pond, during his permanency in that city, met and admired Ghezzi, and when a few years later after his return to England he decided to engrave twenty-five caricatures from drawings of foreign artists twelve were from works by Ghezzi, the only contemporary painter included in the selection. This publication was well received and decisively increased the interest for such art in that country not only among intellectuals and collectors but also reached some of the more perceptive representatives of the English ruling class. This class, only one per cent of British and Irish citizens of the period whose members were connected by birth, schooling, marriage, club and political alliances,[2] also comprised the vast majority of those who undertook the 'Grand Tour'. For some of them, used to the pungent and moralistic satire of Hogarth's prints, the impact of Ghezzi's playfully ironic images in Rome would seem more appealing and enjoyable and if, to this, we add also that the genre was very much in vogue among the Italian and French aristocracy of the time, we have all the reasons for its immediate success with the Irish and British Grand Tourists.

In 1751, when the Leesons and Joseph Henry had been drawn by Ghezzi a number of times, they were the first to show the same appreciation by approaching the young Reynolds to caricature them and their friends in a series of canvases. Their example was immediately followed by fellow Grand Tourists of the same contingent who obtained more pictures of the kind from the artist.[3] Later in his life, Reynolds clearly regretted having produced this type of work, while instead it was successfully pursued by Thomas Patch who fulfilled the demands of the many British and Irish travellers after establishing himself in Florence.[4]

1 Mahon 1947, pp.259-64, notes 43-48.
2 Valentine 1970, p.XI.
3 In July 1751, Diderot, in the first edition of his *Encyclopèdie*, observed:'c'est une espece de libertinage d'imagination qu'il ne faut se permettre tout au plus que par délassement' (*Encyclopèdie ou Dictionnaire des sciences, des arts et des métiers, par une société de gens de lettres*, vol. II, Paris, 1751).
4 It appears that Patch (probably in 1750) painted a caricature of Irish and British travellers in Rome in which were included among others, Lord Charlemont, Lord Bruce and Charles Turner (Royal Irish Academy [RIA] Charlemont MSS 12. R. 20, no. 58.) see p.50, note 8.

Fig. 6 PierLeone Ghezzi, Sir Thomas Kennedy and John Ward, *pen and brown ink on paper, formerly Cranbedok Academy of Art, Bloomfield Hills, Michigan*

the Caricatures

PIER LEONE GHEZZI (1674-1755)

15 *John Martin, Joseph Henry, Lord Bruce of Tottenham and Lord Midleton*

Pen and brown ink, faint traces of black chalk and touches of colour, on light brown laid paper, 32.2 x 22.2 cm
Inscribed on verso in brown ink at upper left: *Henry, Martin, Lord Bruce & Ld Middleton*

Philadelphia Museum of Art: Bequest of Anthony Morris Clark (inv. no.1978-70-289)

16 *Joseph Leeson, later 2nd Earl of Milltown, and Lord Charlemont*

Pen and brown ink, faint traces of black chalk and touches of colour, on light brown laid paper, 32.2 x 22.3 cm
Inscribed on verso in brown ink at upper left: *Leeson & Ld Charlemount*

Philadelphia Museum of Art: Bequest of Anthony Morris Clark (inv. no. 978-70-290)

Provenance: H.D. Molesworth, London; Hans Calman, London, 1962; bequeathed by Anthony Morris Clark

The notoriety achieved by Pier Leone Ghezzi in his time as an unrivalled and brilliant caricaturist is still very strong today and partially casts a shadow on his ability as a painter for which he was also highly commended.[1] Son and grandson of renowned artists, he inherited the same talent. From his father he was forced to draw only with a pen so he could not make changes or corrections.[2] Throughout his life he was involved in multifarious activities. He was surveyor of the papal collections and official evaluator of some public artistic commissions. In 1710 he was created *Cavaliere* by the Duke of Parma.[3] As an artist he was also a skilful engraver and an excellent producer of designs and decorations for scenery to celebrate important events, like those made in 1729 in Piazza Navona to celebrate the birth of a new heir to the throne of France which are recorded in a large painting by Giovanni Paolo Panini, one version of which is now in the National Gallery of Ireland.[4] On that occasion, Ghezzi was rewarded for his achievement with a diamond worth 200 Roman *scudi* by the Cardinal Melchior de Polignac, then French ambassador in Rome.[5] He became a perfect acquaintance for many Irish and British Grand Tourists who were anxious to polish their taste and their education.[6]

Throughout his life, Ghezzi showed an uncommon gift as a satirical draughtsman which he used to demonstrate daily in innumerable portraits of people of every rank and nationality. So strong was this inclination that the artist did not hesitate to caricature even the Pope, Benedetto XIII, on his deathbed.[7]

In the Philadelphia caricatures, some of these gentlemen are shown engaged in one of their more frequent daily activities, taking tea in their lodgings or in one of the popular 'coffee-houses' located around Piazza di Spagna. There, they could catch up on what was happening at home by reading the newspapers which were sent from London almost on a regular basis.

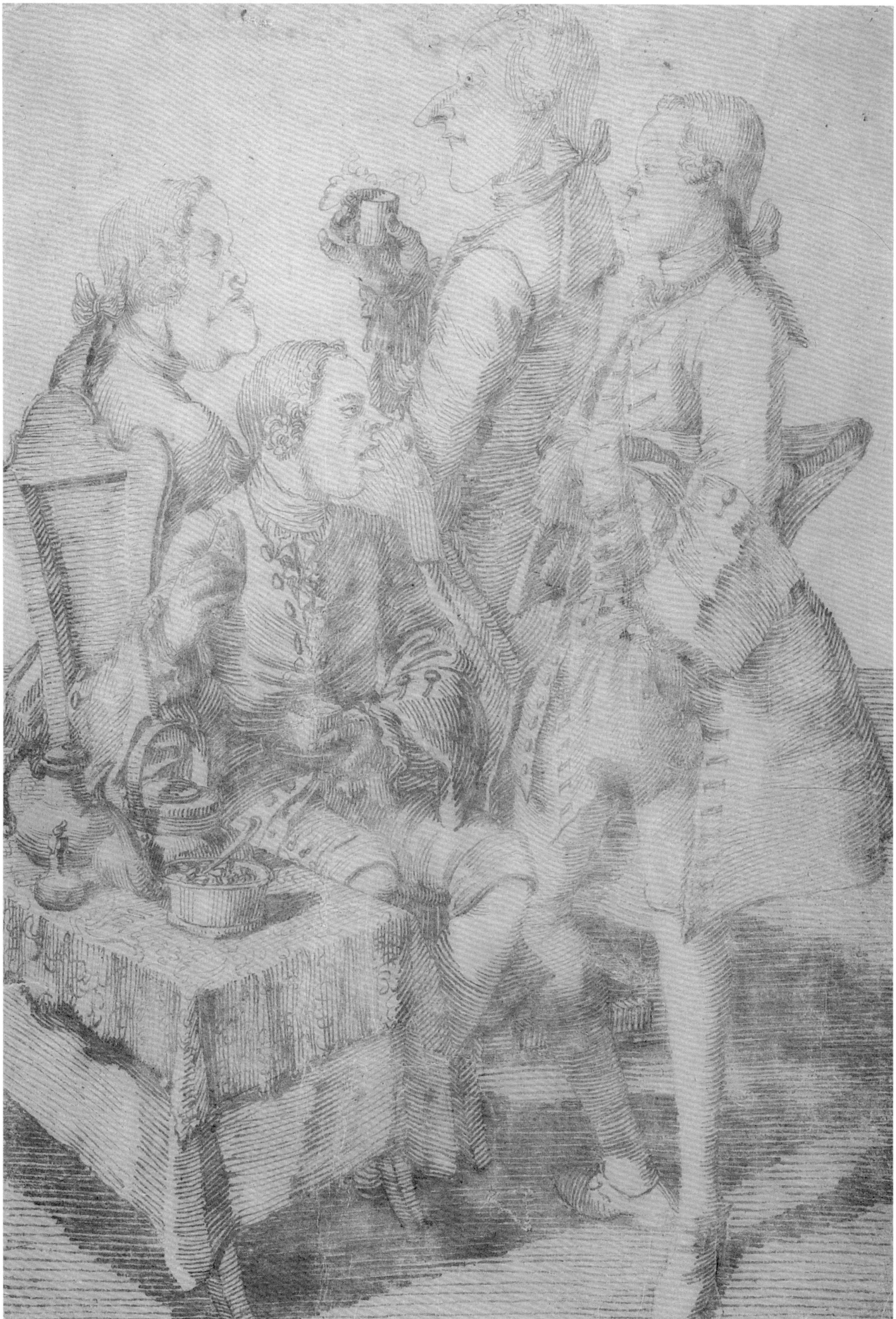

15

In the first, Joseph Henry of Straffan, nephew of Joseph Leeson, is seated at the front. His distinctive features were recorded by Ghezzi in several other drawings in one of which (fig. 5) he stands among some classical ruins with a book on Roma Antica in his hands, most probably the updated edition of Gregorio Roisecco's widely used guide to Rome.[8] Henry's knowledge of antiquity was apparently sincerely esteemed by Ghezzi who described him in two of these caricatures, *V° Giuseppe Henry Inglese huomo assai erudito nelle antichità .. .*[9] (figs. 5 and 9), confirming the reputation he held at home.

Seated behind Henry is John Martin of whom we know very little and that is in connection with the man in front of him, Thomas Bruce-Brudenell, Baron of Tottenham.[10] A good friend of Lord Charlemont, Lord Bruce spent two years in Italy and was included in two of Reynolds' caricatures (nos. 19 and 21) and in the Yale conversation piece (no. 18). The fourth gentleman who stands on the right is George Brodrick, 3rd Viscount of Midleton, another associate of James Caulfield (Lord Charlemont).[11]

In the second caricature we find Joseph Leeson drinking tea on the left and Lord Charlemont on the right, cutting a slice of bread. Ghezzi portrayed the young Leeson on one more occasion (fig. 7).

Of all the caricatures drawn by Ghezzi of the Leesons and their friends, three previously unpublished works are clearly dated to the last months of 1750 and it is probable that all the rest of the caricatures were made around the same time.

Fig. 7 Pier Leone Ghezzi, Joseph Leeson, *1750, Istituto Nazionale per la Grafica, Rome*

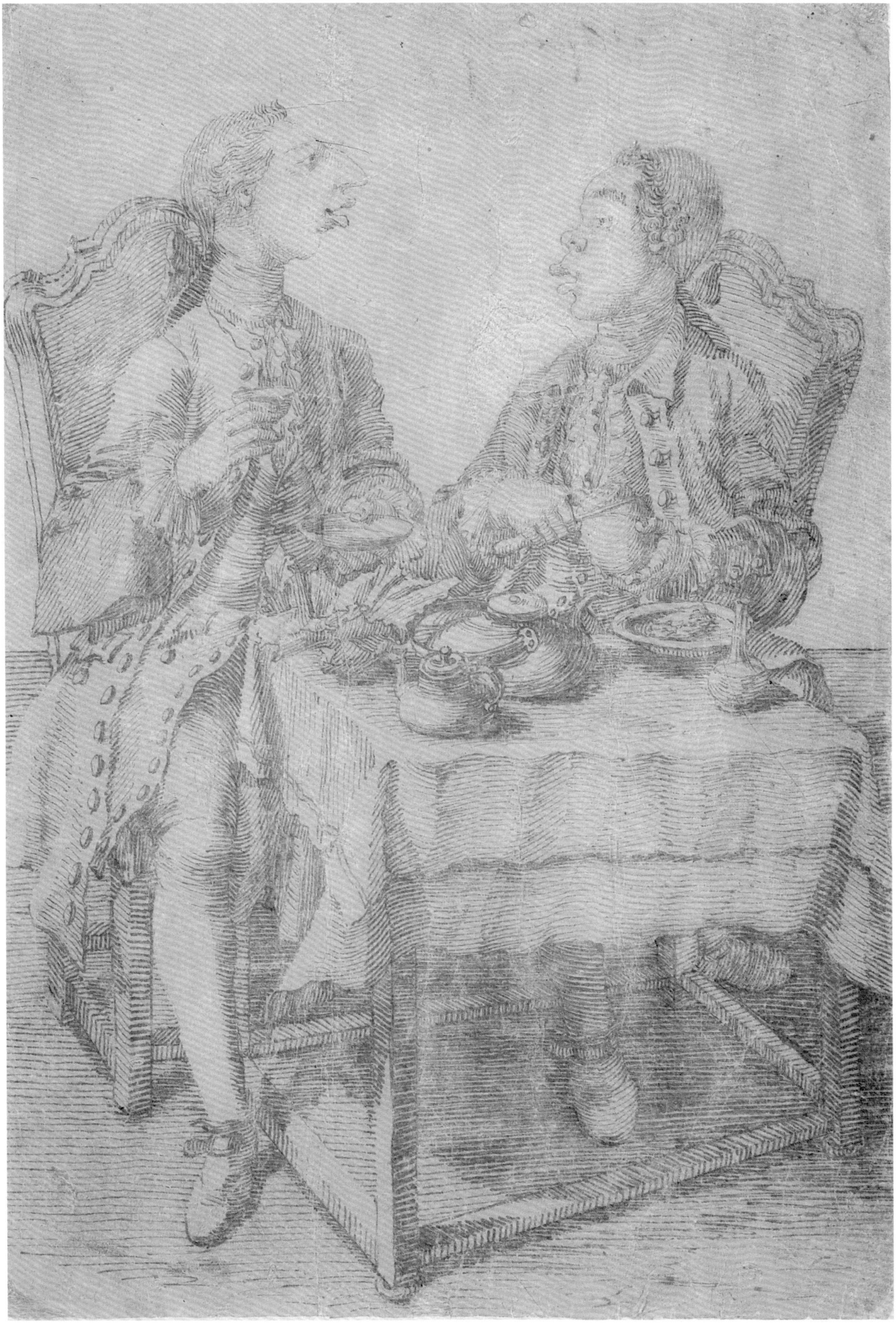

16

1. The most complete work on the artist is Lo Bianco 1985.
2. See Pio Ms. 1977, p.155.
3. Lo Bianco 1985, p.95.
4. NGI inv. no. 95.
5. *Diario Ordinario*, 24 December 1729, no. 1933.
6. For Ghezzi's drawings see Bodart 1976.
7. Lo Bianco 1985, p.97.
8. Gregorio Roisecco, *Roma antica e moderna o sia nuova descrizione di tutti gl'edifici antichi, e moderni . . .*, Rome 1750.
9. He is described as: *V.º Giuseppe Henry Inglese huomo assai erudito nelle antichità e in Letteratura huomo assai ...*', in the drawing in the Metropolitan Museum of Art, New York (Rogers Fund, 1973). Originally, it was bound in a book of caricatures, one of three looted by the Duke of Wellington after the battle of Victoria in 1813 during the Peninsular Campaign.
10. 'John Martin jun. Esq. of Overbury, in the County of Worcester ', 26 September 1751, Lucca, Charlemont Manuscripts, 1: 183-88 (information resarched by Cynthia O'Connor). Probably he is one and the same man who is recorded passing through Capua on 13 April 1752: see Ingamells 1997, p.646.
11. Ingamells 1997, pp.146-47.
12. These three are all in the collection of the Istituto Nazionale per la Grafica, in Rome, and they have these inscriptions:
    a) *Monsieur Lisson Inglese fatto dà Mè Cav.re Ghezzi 27 8bre - 1750*. (FN 19843)
    b) *V.º Giuseppe Henry Inglese huomo assai erudito nelle antichità 9bre 1750*, and lower, *partito dà Roma per Venetia li 12 Maggio 1751*. (FN 4739)
    c) *Mons.r Henry fatto dà Mè Ghezzi, 27 Xbre 50*. (FN 4738)

Essential Literature: Bowron 1980, pp.24-26; Godfrey 1984, pp.31-32; Clark 1985, p.250; Bean and Griswold 1990, pp.86-87.

*Fig. 8 Pier Leone Ghezzi, Joseph Henry, 1750,
Istituto Nazionale per la Grafica, Rome*

*Fig. 9 Pier Leone Ghezzi, Joseph Henry, 1750,
Istituto Nazionale per la Grafica, Rome*

ANONYMOUS *after* PIER LEONE GHEZZI

17 *John Leeson, later 2nd Earl of Milltown, and Lord Charlemont*

Pen and iron gall ink on antique laid paper, 36 x 26 cm

Private Collection

Provenance: by descent in the Clements family

This caricature closely repeats no. 16, and for a long time it has been considered as by the hand of Pier Leone Ghezzi.[1] Although almost identical to the other, this drawing does not carry the same crispness and liveliness of the original described above.[2] Its importance, however, rests in its historical provenance. In the eighteenth century the family who own this drawing was one of the most important in Ireland and enjoyed well documented, cordial relations with both the Milltowns and the Charlemonts. It is quite possible, therefore, that the original Ghezzi drawing was copied at the request of the ancestors of the current owner or otherwise received by them as a gift.[3] If this suggestion is correct, it would then appear that the original Ghezzi drawings were acquired and brought back to Ireland after the Grand Tour by either Lord Charlemont or Joseph Leeson, which seems quite a plausible hypothesis.

1 Wynne 1974, p.109, fig.13, proposed the identification of the second sitter as Joseph Henry, and erroneously believed that the drawing was originally in the Milltown Collection.
2 Anthony Clark was the first to question its authenticity in a letter dated 6 March 1974 (NGI Archive). After him, Edgar Peters Bowron also refuted the attribution to Pier Leone Ghezzi in Bowron 1980, p.26.
3 In the same collection there is also a copy of Reynolds' caricature, no. 21 (NGI inv. no.736).

17

BRITISH ARTIST, *probably* THOMAS PATCH (1725-1782)

18 *Connoisseurs in Rome, 1751*

Oil on canvas, 94.5 x 134.5 cm

Yale Center for British Art, Paul Mellon Collection

Provenance: Sir Charles Turner, Kirkleatham Hall; Mrs Leroy Lewis, sold Sotheby's London, 23 March 1949 (lot 42, as by Reynolds) bought by Agnew; The Hon. Nellie Ionides by 1955, sold Sotheby's London, 29 May 1963 (lot 93, as Nathaniel Dance), bought by Agnew for Paul Mellon

Connoisseurs in Rome has been described as one of the most emblematic representations of the Grand Tour. In front of one of the most famous settings in Rome, this group of gentlemen pose with all the pride and confidence that befits their status, pretending to be absorbed in making erudite observations of the surrounding ancient monuments. All the more surprising then to learn that even though the sitters were carefully portrayed neither their identification nor the author of the composition has ever been satisfactorily resolved. Denys Sutton, who was the first to call attention to this canvas, rightly suggested its possible link with Reynolds' *Parody of the 'School of Athens'*.[1] He also made the first attempt to recognise the sitters proposing a set of names which in part were correct. By comparing certain features with some of the known people in the Milltown caricatures, Sutton proved the presence in this picture of Sir Thomas Kennedy and Lord Charlemont on the left, and Sir William Lowther in the centre. He also logically guessed that Charles Turner should be among the other figures, since the painting was recorded to have come from his known residence of Kirkleatham Hall.[2]

When the canvas was recently exhibited in London and Rome, Hugh Belsey in the catalogue referred to Charles Turner as the small gentleman in the centre, leaning on an architectural fragment.[3] A quick look at Turner's features in two of the caricatures painted by Reynolds confirms the correctness of that proposal (no. 23, and fig. 23) which leaves only the two gentlemen on the far right without a proper identity.

The man with fair hair, although seated, appears to be very tall. His pronounced facial profile also provides a clue as to who he could be, but it is his red frock-coat with its rich embroidery and dark lining which permits us to here recognise him as Thomas Bruce-Brudenell of Tottenham, one of Lord Charlemont's closest friends. He wears exactly the same costume in Reynolds' caricatures (nos. 19 and 21).

The final figure, indicating the Arch of Constantine with his left hand, is instead an unexpected member of the Irish and British contingent in Rome at that time, Thomas Steavens.[4] His identification is unchallengeable, since a portrait of him exists in a private collection (fig. 10) from which this image precisely derives.

Steavens, another friend of Lord Charlemont, undertook an extended Grand Tour. It is interesting to note that at least three of the people portrayed here were well-known 'buddies' of James Caulfield and that the remaining two, Sir William Lowther and Charles Turner, were at least well acquainted with him.[5]

18

Fig. 10 British School 18th century, Thomas Steavens, *ca. 1751, oil on canvas, private collection*

With regard to the authorship of the painting several names have been advanced, including some which today appear quite surprising.[6] The most promising attribution was that to James Russell, initially proposed by Denys Sutton and recently restated.[7] Undoubtedly the author's name should emerge from the narrow circle of British artist-dealers who were rambling around these aristocrats, and I believe that another possibility should be explored. One very interesting hint in this regard came to light some years ago with a reference to a caricature which Thomas Patch was supposed to have painted for Charles Turner, and which included also Lord Charlemont and Lord Bruce.[8] In a sense, this painter could be the perfect candidate for the Yale work: it is known that he maintained the best relations with every one of the sitters.[9] Moreover, the monumental background of the composition shows mannerisms of a typical professional landscape painter, as Patch was, and it is evident that whoever made this picture had difficulty assembling the figures proportionally, most certainly for want of experience.[10] Regrettably, we know very little about Thomas Patch's ability as a realistic portraitist and his later successful activity as a caricaturist cannot be of any assistance.

One final word should be said about the possible date of this painting. All the gentlemen portrayed spent very long periods in the Holy City but only in the early months of 1751 could they have been together, and it seems quite plausible that this picture was at least started at the same time as Reynolds' *Parody*.[11]

1 Sutton 1956, p.117.

2 *Ibidem*.

3 Wilton and Bignamini 1996, p.88, no.43.

4 Thomas Steavens (*ca*.1728-1759) was the son of a Baronet and rich timber merchant, and brother-in-law of the antiquarian James West of Alscot Park. In 1747, at the beginning of his Grand Tour he was for *ca*. two years secretary to Sir Charles Hanbury-Williams, British Envoy in Dresden, who described him as 'an exceedingly good scholar, with very good parts and a very good estate' (see Earl of Ilchester 1928, pp.160-61). In 1751, he was nominated a member of the Society of Dilettanti. He was constantly in Italy from the summer of 1749 until October 1756 with only one interruption, from early summer 1751 to the beginning of 1753.

5 Lord Bruce and Sir Thomas Kennedy were founding Promoters of Lord Charlemont's 'Academy of British Painters in Rome'. Thomas Steavens was described as being loyal to Lord Charlemont (Charlemont Manuscripts, 1:200).

6 As by Joshua Reynolds (lot. 42, Sotheby's, 23 March 1949) and as Nathaniel Dance (lot 93, 29 May 1963).

7 Sutton 1956, *loc. cit.*; Belsey in Wilton and Bignamini 1996, *loc. cit.*.

8 'I hope Lord Caulfield found time to see our Caricatures by Patch I believe which was bought by an upper servant at the sale of the Late S.r C. Turner's who will not part with it to me without the present Sr Charles consent which I cannot get', RIA, Charlemont MSS 12.R.20, no. 58, 12 January 1799. This information was first communicated by Cynthia O'Connor in 1983, p.18.

9 Thomas Patch painted landscapes for Lord Charlemont and purchased a Claude Lorrain landscape, formerly in the Muti Collection in Rome, for Sir William Lowther (see Russell 1975, pp.115-19). Thomas Steavens gave letters of recommendation to Patch for Sir Horace Mann, Lord Huntingdon and others in Florence when, in January 1756, the painter was banned from Rome (see Watson 1939-1940, p.20).

10 The composition of the group seems to have originated in individual sketched portraits and only later assembled together. If we compare the figures of Turner and Lowther with those in Reynolds' caricature at Holker Hall (no. 23), it is evident that their difference in height is completely misrepresented. This error of proportion has also created some confusion in their identification and Turner's figure was believed to be instead Ralph Howard of Shelton Abbey (see C. O'Connor in Ingamells 1997, p.529). Howard arrived in Rome at the earliest in the winter 1751-52 at which time Thomas Steavens was already in France. It should be noted that Lord Charlemont is positioned with his back to the Colosseum. Pompeo Batoni later used the same monument as the background to his only one known portrait (of two) of James Caulfield.

11 I suspect that the connection of this picture with the *Parody* is stronger than at first appears, and that it preceded the Reynolds by a short time. It should also be said that both paintings are the same size.

Essential Literature: Sutton 1956, *loc. cit.*; Nygren and Pressly 1977, p.28, no.30; Belsey in Wilton and Bignamini 1996, *loc. cit.*.

JOSHUA REYNOLDS (1723-1792)

19 *Parody on the 'School of Athens', 1751*

Oil on canvas, 96.5 x 133.5 cm

Inscription repeated from the original on the relined canvas: *Joseph Henry (Reynolds Pinx: ¹) Romæ 1751*

National Gallery of Ireland (inv. no. 734)

Provenance: Joseph Henry of Straffan; by descent; Christie's sale, 14 March 1868, lot 168, where bought in for 190 guineas and subsequently sold as property of Trustees of a Charitable Institution at Foster's, 25 May 1870, lot 114, for £105, to Lady Barbara Countess of Milltown; Earls of Milltown; Milltown Gift 1902 (no. 230, Deed of Gift).

Reynolds went to Italy at the first opportunity which arose for him. He left England in 1749 as part of a naval mission dispatched to the Mediterranean and, having spent the second half of the year in Minorca, he sailed for Livorno in January 1750. He arrived in Rome the following April and remained there for two years. He was twenty-seven and in Rome he decided to dedicate himself completely to the study of ancient statuary and the 'old masters'. Thus resolved, he probably never painted any portraits there until he agreed to produce a number of caricatures for the Leesons and their friends.[1]

The *Parody*, as we know, was commissioned by Joseph Henry, the most erudite in classics of the entire Irish and British contingent at that time in Rome. We should not be surprised, therefore, if the content of this picture was required to be more elaborate then that of any other caricature. We cannot say if the choice of the setting came from Henry, and actually it is more probable that it was Reynolds' idea, but we should not exclude the possibility that Henry had some input in the composition.

It is known that Reynolds spent a lot of time in Raphael's 'Stanze' in the Vatican. There he made sketches of single heads and also copied in oil the 'School of Athens'.[2] When a new edition of Bellori's treatise on Raphael's works in the Vatican Palace was published in 1751 Reynolds owned and annotated a copy which is now in Harvard College.[3]

In creating the scenery he placed the *Parody* in a gothic surrounding and, since the use of the word 'gothic' for Italian art theorists was always synonymous with 'barbaric', in that way he ridiculed the taste and the northern origins of his fellow connoisseurs.[4] He replaced the Greek Gods in the architectural niches with Carnival masks. Then, in a sequence of burlesque analogies with Raphael's composition, he assigned to each of his open-minded *Milordi* the position of a philosopher or a mathematician. Reynolds kept almost a complete record of the sitters' names in one of his Roman sketch-books, but in a random order. Previous studies were significant in identifying many of the people represented in the painting, but now we are perhaps able to add a few more names.[5]

In the foreground group on the left (no. 19a), where Raphael had portrayed Pythagoras surrounded by his students, elaborating the harmonic proportions of music, Sir Thomas Kennedy (fig. 12) plays the transverse flute, Lord Charlemont with the recorder sits next to him (fig. 13) and Richard

19

Fig. 11 *Parody's Sitters*

1 Sir Thomas Kennedy 2 Lord Charlemont 3 Richard Phelps 4 Sir Matthew Fetherstonaugh 5 Matthew Brettingham 6 Simon Vierpyl 7 Lord Bruce of Tottenham
8 Thomas Barrett-Lennard 9 Lascelles Iremonger 10 Benjamin Lethieullier 11 Sir William Lowther 12 Joseph Leeson Senior 13 ? Robert Maxwell 14 William Bagot
15 Joseph Leeson Junior 16 Abbè Dubois 17 ? Mr Sterling 18 Thomas Dawson 19 Dr James Irwin 20 Thomas Patch 21 Revd Edward Murphy 22 Joseph Henry * Idea Figures

19a

Fig. 12 Pompeo Batoni, Sir Thomas Kennedy, 1764, oil on canvas, National Trust for Scotland

Fig. 13 Pompeo Batoni, James Caulfield, later 1st Earl of Charlemont, 1753-55, oil on canvas, Yale Center for British Art, Paul Mellon Collection

Fig. 14 Pompeo Batoni, Sir Matthew Fetherstonhaugh, 1751, oil on canvas, The National Trust, Uppark

Phelps plays the cello. Behind them, holding the sheet music, is Sir Matthew Fetherstonhaugh (fig. 14).[6] Above them, on the far left, where the servants were in the 'School of Athens', are two artist-dealers, Matthew Brettingham carrying a large portfolio, and Simon Vierpyl (no. 19b).[7]

Moving to the right there are two figures contrasting in height: these are Lord Bruce of Tottenham and Thomas Barrett-Lennard (no. 19c and fig. 15), replacing Alcibiades and Socrates.[8]

In the centre, where the two major philosophers Plato and Aristotle were supposed to be we find instead that the first is impersonated by the corpulent figure of Joseph Leeson Senior, and behind him his 'audience' comprises Sir William Lowther, Benjamin Lethieullier and Lascelles Iremonger (no. 19c and figs. 16-18).[9] It is not clear who is the person taking the role of Aristotle, who seems to be in a heated argument with Leeson, nor can we yet identify the small man behind him.[10] Instead, the tall slim person with the aquiline nose, is certainly Joseph Leeson Junior (no. 19d).

Moving again to the right, four more figures are portrayed: three are almost certainly 'idea figures', as Reynolds recorded them, while the fourth wearing a dark brown frock-coat and deep in writing is Abbé Dubois.[11]

In the lower group on the right, where in the Raphael Euclid is explaining some principle of geometry to his students, the mathematician is replaced by the 'jolly' Dr Irwin (fig. 19), who is busy taking the circumference of a large loaf of bread with a compass, ignoring the two dogs sniffing around (no. 19e).[12] Beside him is probably Thomas Dawson (fig. 20), and the figure standing behind could be the mysterious Mr Sterling.[13] As for the last two people on the right, also standing, the one seen from behind with a fan in his hand is the last of the four 'idea figures', while the other is Thomas Patch who appropriately occupies the place of the painter Sodoma in Raphael's fresco.[14]

Sitting in the centre foreground, taking notes or writing accounts, is the Reverend Edward Murphy, major-domo of Lord Charlemont.[15] Finally, lying on the steps, with a pile of books beside him, the owner the painting, Joseph Henry himself, is portrayed posing like Diogenes the Cynic, in contempt of any ostentation, reading a scarcely intellectual novel entitled Larry Grog.[16]

As we know from the inscription on the reverse, the *Parody* was painted in 1751, but we can be even more precise adding that it was not started before 19 January of that year.[17]

1 See Penny 1986, pp.20-21.

2 Reynolds caught a chill in the Vatican in the winter which caused his later deafness, see Malone in Reynolds 1798, vol. 1, p.LXXXVIII. The copy was recorded by Graves and Cronin 1899, vol. III, p.1245. The canvas was on the London market twice, in Sotheby's, 9 July 1980, lot 63 and Christie's, 16 July 1982, lot 67.

3 Bellori 1751; Wind 1949.

4 The meaning of the word was clear also to the more sophisticated of the Grand Tourists as Cynthia O'Connor 1983, p.20 proved.

5 Sutton 1956, pp.115-17; O'Connor 1983, pp.4-22.

6 The group is practically the same as no. 22, with the addition of Sir Matthew Fetherstonhaugh (1714-1774) of Uppark. He was married to Sarah Lethieullier and together they travelled in Italy in 1750-51. During their trip they met and for sometime travelled with Benjamin Lethieullier and Lascelles Iremonger, brother and half-brother of Lady Sarah. In 1751 he and his wife sat twice for Batoni for their portraits. Lady Sarah also sat for another one with her brother Lethieullier. Sir Matthew's purchases in Italy included landscapes from Vernet and scagliola table-tops from Pietro Belloni. See Ingamells 1997, p.354, and Clark 1985, pp.252-54.

19b

19c

Fig. 15 Pompeo Batoni, Thomas Barrett-Lennard, *1750, oil on canvas, private collection*

Fig. 16 Pompeo Batoni, Lascelles Iremonger, *1751, oil on canvas, The National Trust, Uppark*

Fig. 17 Pompeo Batoni, Benjamin Lethieullier, *1751, oil on canvas, The National Trust, Uppark*

Fig. 18 Sir Joshua Reynolds, Sir William Lowther, *oil on canvas, The Trustees of the Holker Estate Trust*

7   Matthew Brettingham (1725-1803) was an architect. From 1747 to 1754 he was in Rome acting also as a dealer. His identification was first made by Cynthia O'Connor when referring to a letter in which he was described as the 'little Architect': see O'Connor 1983, p.12. The suggestion that the other man could be only Simon Vierpyl (ca.1725-1810) is based on his place in the composition. Of him we know only one other portrait, included in a group of gentlemen, painted by J. Trotter for the Bluecoat School in Dublin.

8   Thomas Barrett-Lennard (1717-1786) of Belhus went to Italy with his wife after the death of their infant daughter, Barbara Anne. He was there from 1749 to 1751. Later in 1755 he became Baron Dacre. His portrait with his wife and their dead daughter painted by Batoni, with the help of a miniature, is one of the most moving pictures by the artist: see Ingamells 1997, pp.53-54 and Clark 1985, pp.246-47.

9   Recently in Hugh Belsey's entry (in Wilton and Bignamini 1996, p.84, no.40) the identity of the two philosophers were mistakenly inverted. As with Joseph Leeson Senior, the figure of Sir William Lowther is repeated by Reynolds from the other smaller caricatures. Instead the tall bare-headed gentleman is Benjamin Lethieullier (1729-1797) of Belmont. Although his name does not appear in Reynolds' list, his resemblance with his portraits make his identification certain. He was the son of the Director of the Bank of England. With his inseparable half-brother, Lascelles R. Iremonger (1718/9-1793) painted beside him, he travelled for two years in Italy. They both sat for Batoni, and purchased landscapes from Vernet. Lethieullier also shared, with Thomas Steavens, the same kind of affection for a lady called Ancilla: see Ingamells 1997, pp.542-34 and 598 and Clark 1985, pp.253-54. See also Black 1992, pp.192-94.

10 In my opinion the only possible candidate for the role of Aristotle should be Mr Maxwell, as his name was listed by Reynolds. Regrettably we know very little about him and no portrait has yet been found. From Cynthia O'Connor's research (1983, p.11), he was considered, with Leeson Senior and Mr. Benson (Ralph Howard's bear-leader), an Irish connoisseur. Objectively, considering his rank, I believe Mr Maxwell was Robert Maxwell (1721-1779) of Farnham, Co. Cavan. In 1759 he succeeded his father as 2nd Baron Farnham, in 1760 he was created Viscount and three years later, Earl of Farnham. For the other small gentleman near by, the best option is William Bagot (1728-1798). He arrived in Rome in January 1751, and was one the best supporters of Lord Charlemont's Academy. He became Baron Bagot, succeeding his father. He purchased important seventeenth-century Italian paintings, and for his entire life he remained passionate about Italy. See Ingamells 1997, p.40.

11 Reynolds mentioned in his list *'Four idea figures'*, meaning the inclusion in the setting of four invented images. Abbé Dubois appears to have been Lord Charlemont's French teacher (see O'Connor 1983, p.12). He is sometimes confused with Jean-Baptiste Dubos (1670-1742), critic and historian, also abbot, who wrote between 1719 and 1733, *Reflexions critiques sur la poésie et la peinture*.

12 Dr James Irwin (ca.1687-1759) spent almost thirty years in Rome. A Scot by birth, he appears to have been a very enjoyable companion for many British Grand Tourists in spite of his Jacobean views. Robert Adam, who remembered him with sympathy, said that every day he used to drink four or five bottles of wine: see Ingamells 1997, pp.545-46.

13 Thomas Dawson (1725-1813), of Co. Monaghan and Dublin, was the son of a banker and Alderman of the City of Dublin. It is not certain how long he was in Rome but we know he was portrayed by Batoni and commissioned landscapes from Vernet. In a letter written by Dr James Tyrrell to Ralph Howard, he is described as 'honest Dawson' (Wicklow Papers, 7 September 1752, NLI). On Mr Sterling nothing has yet been found, but his name may have been misspelled by Reynolds.

14 Thomas Patch (1725-1782), painter and dealer, arrived in Rome in 1747. There he lived in Casa Zuccari and for a short time above the *Caffè degli Inglesi* in Piazza di Spagna. He studied with Vernet and painted copies of his works. Like all the other artists he dealt in works of art. His hot-temperament created many problems for him. Probably known to be a paedophile by most of the British and Irish community, he was expelled from Rome in 1755 by the 'Santo Uffizio' for this crime. He recovered in Florence where he progressed successfully as a landscape painter and caricaturist. It is clear that Reynolds and Henry knew Patch's vice and that is why he was placed in the same position as another notorious paedophile, Giovanni Antonio Bazzi, better known as 'il Sodoma'. See Watson 1939-1940, pp.15-50 and Russell 1975, pp.115-19.

15 Edward Murphy (1707-1777) was tutor and major-domo to Lord Charlemont, and he travelled with him from 1746 to 1754. A classical scholar, he was a loyal and efficient companion to James Caulfield: see O'Connor in Ingamells 1997, pp.687-88.

16 *Ibidem*, p.484.

17 This *terminus ante quem* is provided by the established date of the arrival of William Bagot in Rome which was on 19 January 1951.

Essential Literature: Graves and Cronin 1989, pp.1230-31; Wind 1949, pp. 294-97; Sutton 1956, pp.115-17; Wynne 1974, p.110; O'Connor 1983, pp.5- 22; Belsey 1996, p.84, no.40.

19d

Fig. 19 Domenico Dupra, Dr James Irwin, 1739, oil on canvas, Scottish National Portrait Gallery

Fig. 20 Pompeo Batoni, Thomas Dawson, 1751, oil on canvas, private collection

19e

JOSHUA REYNOLDS (1723-1792)

20 *Joseph Leeson* later **1st Earl of Milltown and Sir William Lowther, 1751**

Oil on canvas, 78 x 51.7 cm (painted surface 76.5 x 49.5 cm)

National Gallery of Ireland (inv. no. 735)

21 **Lord Bruce, John Ward, Joseph Leeson Jnr and Joseph Henry, 1751**

Oil on canvas, 64 x 49.5 cm

National Gallery of Ireland (inv. no. 736)

22 **Sir Thomas Kennedy, Lord Charlemont, John Ward and Richard Phelps, 1751**

Oil on canvas, 64 x 49.5 cm

National Gallery of Ireland (inv. no. 737)

Provenance (for all three): Earls of Milltown (nos. 123, 121, 124, Deed of Gift)

The amazing response to Ghezzi's caricatures among the Irish and British *Milordi* must have convinced Joseph Leeson to secure some of these burlesque images for himself on a larger and more durable scale. We can speculate that he first attempted to persuade the aged Ghezzi who would certainly have considered that genre only as a pastime, and that with his refusal Leeson would resort to using one of the young British painters affiliated to their group. The choice of Joshua Reynolds was most probably made because he was known to be a portraitist, and it is unfortunate that we do not know how he convinced the artist but we can imagine what sort of argument he may have used.[1] We know for sure that after this episode Reynolds never again attempted to paint caricatures and that later he expressed his regret to his pupils.[2]

The fact that Leeson was the first to obtain these pictures can be proved by some observations. In staging the *Parody*, Reynolds has evidently tried to make the best use of the three conversation pieces just painted for Leeson. He integrated the figures of the first where necessary into the new one. But in the case of Joseph Lesson Senior, for some reason unknown to us, he decided to reverse the bulky shape of the wealthy Irishman forgetting that in such a way Leeson would appear abnormally holding his quizzing glass with his left hand.[3] On a more technical point, the small caricatures are painted in a more refined manner and although executed with a fast brushwork they show a better impasto which cannot be explained just by their evident better condition. Several *pentimenti* are visible in the *Parody*, and they are the result of subsequent additions to the composition, of figures or objects. In the other pictures, instead, where the changes appear, they

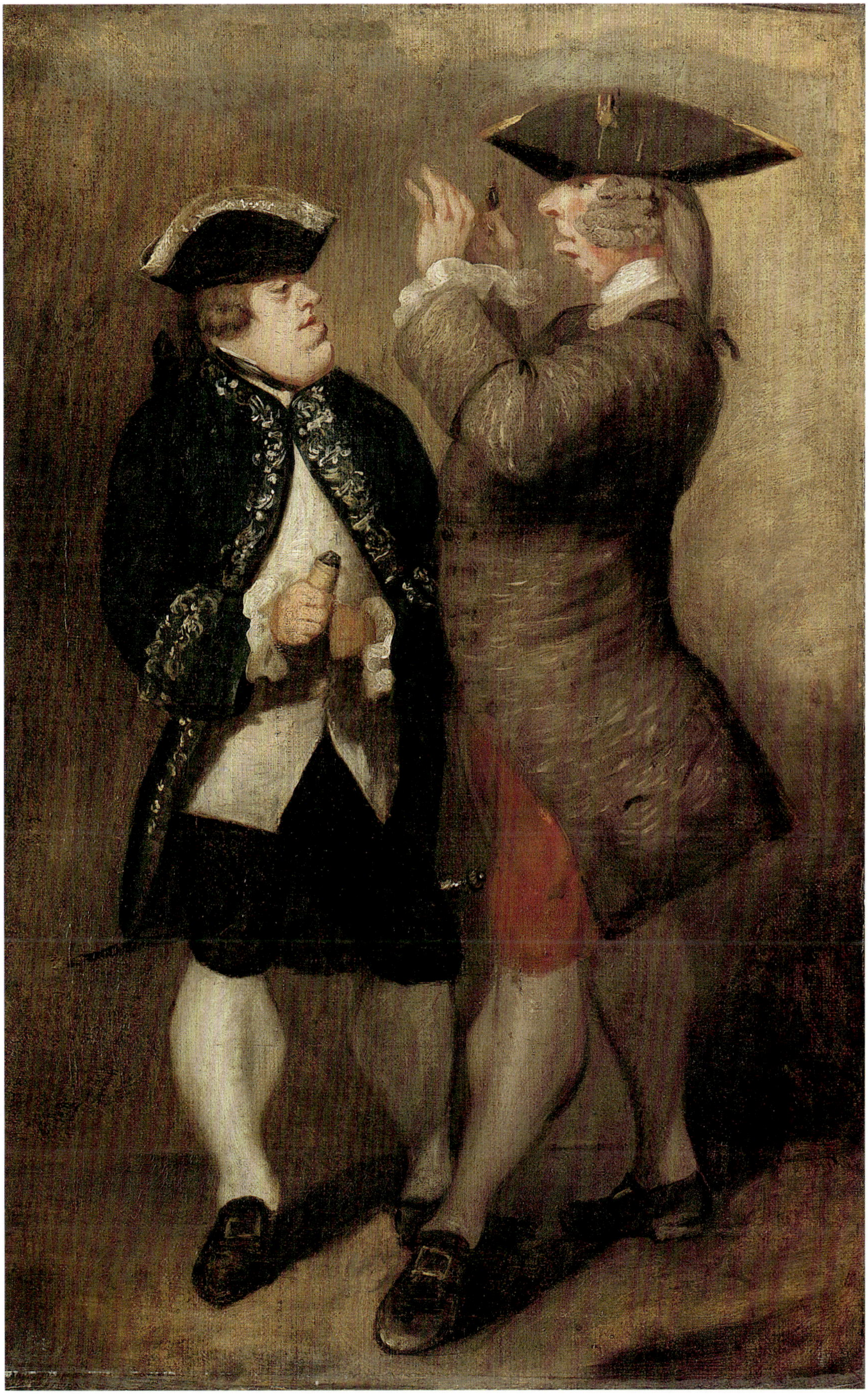

20

comprise real differences of gestures or actions. Even though in such cases it is not an easy task to propose a chronology we can deduce that the three conversation pieces should be contemporary or just a fraction earlier than the works from Holker Hall and Rhode Island (fig. 22), and precede the *Parody* by a short time, while the *Escapade of Ralph Howard*, as we know, was painted one year later.[4]

Each one of these pictures carries some ironic comment on the daily habits of the sitters. In the first we observe the tall and massive figure of Joseph Leeson pretending to be capable of judging the authenticity of a medal or a gem hidden in his left hand with his magnified glass. Before him is Sir William Lowther, physically not very attractive, but certainly a good and generous listener.[5]

In the group portrayed in the second caricature the giraffe-like figure of Lord Bruce reads a poem or perhaps a quotation to the young Joseph Leeson and to the Hon. John Ward of Hamlet, who was also remembered for 'his Classics in his pocket and quoting his authors'.[6] In the background, usually neglected by Reynolds, a fountain like one of those designed by Bernini for St. Peter's Square is painted. Joseph Henry instead, seated with his books, seems to be completely occupied in his study which in this particular case, was of ancient sewers.

In the third and final canvas, Ward is shown again, this time with an ecstatic look, probably provoked by the musical performance of his three friends,[7] and all four wear the symbols of their country on their hats: St Andrew's white-blue cross for Kennedy, green shamrocks for Charlemont, red St George's cross for Ward, and a leek for Phelps.

1 From other episodes, we can imagine that Leeson must have made an offer that Reynolds could not refuse.
2 'I have heard Sir Joshua himself declare, that, although it was universally allowed he executed subjects of this kind with much humour and spirit, he held it absolutely necessary to abandon the practice, since it must corrupt his taste as portrait painter, whose duty it becomes to aim at discovering the perfections and not the imperfections of those he is to represent ', Northcote 1817, p.29.
3 He was probably reversed so as to have him facing a different group.
4 In one of his Roman sketch-books Reynolds listed the caricatures in this order: first, two of those belonging to Leeson, then the one in Holker Hall followed by the one in Rhode Island, and finally the *Parody*. What he did not record was the one with just Leeson and Lowther, which could have been done as a preliminary study for the one in Holker Hall and therefore not considered important enough to mention. He did not record *Ralph Howard's Escapade* probably because the notes for that commission which was finished only in 1752 were taken by him earlier: see O'Connor 1983, pp.7-8.
5 Sir William Lowther (1727-1756) 3rd baronet of Marske, Yorkshire, and of Holker Hall, Lancashire, died unmarried in 1756 and was regretted by many, including Lady Mary Wortley Montague (see Wortley Montague Letters, vol. III, 1967, pp.107-08). In September 1751, in a sort of boyish game, Lord Charlemont and Lord Bruce waged different sums of money on who among a number of their acquaintances in Lucca would die first. Suddenly, William Lowther was among those (Charlemont Manuscripts, vol. 1, pp.183, 4:5).
6 Ingamells 1997, pp.765-66.
7 O'Connor 1983, p.15.

Essential Literature: Graves and Cronin 1989, pp.1230-31; Sutton 1956, pp.115-17; O'Connor 1983, pp.5- 22; Penny 1986, pp.176-77.

21

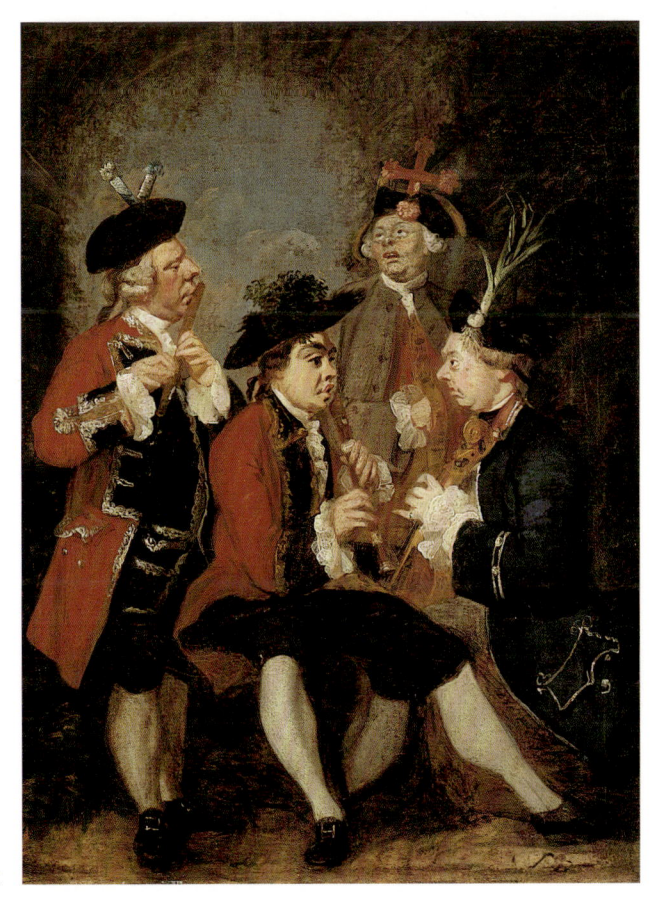

22

JOSHUA REYNOLDS (1723 - 1792)

23 *Charles Turner, Sir William Lowther, Joseph Leeson and Mr Huet with a dog, 1751*

Oil on canvas, 61.6 x 48 cm

The Trustees of the Holker Estate Trust

Provenance: Sir William Lowther of Marske

This caricature was evidently commissioned from Reynolds by Sir William Lowther. The figures of Lowther and Leeson appear to have been repeated precisely but on a slightly smaller scale from one of those painted for Joseph Leeson, which supports the belief that all these canvases were produced by Reynolds at the same time. The satirical appeal is also the same: once again Joseph Leeson Senior seems to be pondering on the quality of a small object hidden in his hand, while the number of his audience has gradually increased.

On the far left is Charles Turner of Kirkleatham, Yorkshire, who became Baronet in 1782, and was known to be very eccentric. He lived relatively near Lowther and from his house came the later copy of this caricature, today in Bowood House, Wiltshire (fig. 21).[1] He also appears holding his ears in another caricature painted by Reynolds for John Woodyeare of Crookhill, another neighbour of his, who instead patiently listens to a duet performed by his tutor Revd Dr Drake and Mr Cook of London (fig. 22).[2]

The last person in this picture is the elderly Mr Huet, of whom we know very little. In a letter written from Siena in the autumn of 1751 he is described relaxing in that town and in the evenings playing *farinacci*.[3]

Several *pentimenti* are detectable. The most evident is perhaps the reduced water jet of the fountain painted on the far right. Looking at the two central figures of the composition, Lowther and Leeson, it seems that Reynolds, who certainly knew Ghezzi's caricatures quite well, has tried to reinterpret one of his famous drawings, now at Chatsworth.[4]

A shepherd dog is seated beside Huet with what appears to be a stone precariously balanced on the tip of his nose. It is not clear who the owner of this dog is and it is more than possible that it was put there, as in the *Parody,* to ridicule the kind of attention these tourists attracted. While wealthy tourists discussing or bargaining over some work of art must been a very common sight around the city, naturally, not all of these 'gentlemen visitors' behaved in the same way or shared the same interests. Some observers were very critical of them and even tried to avoid their company.[5]

1 See Miller 1982, pp.28-29. The painting (59.5 x 49.5 cm) is catalogued as by Reynolds and purchased at Turner's sale by the 3rd Marquis. Strangely, in the Witt Library the same picture is classified as owned by Agnew 1958. An oil caricature, supposedly by Reynolds, was exhibited by Agnew in October-November 1954, and purchased by L.G. Duke (whereabouts unknown). One more mystery is a 'pen and wash' drawing attributed to Reynolds by L.G. Duke, and supposed to be a composition study for the above picture, which is also mentioned by Neilson 1954, n.p., Sutton 1956, pp.115-16, and Miller 1982, p.28, and said to be in the Sir John Soane's Museum in London. However, in response to our enquiry there, it seems now that it was never in that collection.

23

2 Oil on canvas, no 53.349 (61.6 x 48 cm), acquired in 1953 as a gift from Mrs Murray S. Danforth by the Museum of Art, Rhode Island School of Design, Providence: see Neilson 1954.
3 SRO, Ailsa MSS, GD 25/ 9/ Box 28/1, Domenico Valentini to Thomas Kennedy, 4 October 1751. *Farinacci* was a game played with dice marked only on one face (see Vocabolario 1746, vol. II, *ad vocem*).
4 The drawing represents the two famous antiquarians, Baron Philip von Stosch and M. Antonio Sabbatini looking at a medal (The Chatsworth House Trust).
5 In a letter of 4 July 1752 to his friend Sir Charles Hanbury-Williams, Thomas Steavens wrote about events which happened to him in the previous year: 'I staid twelve days at Rome, I did not confirm my health with the English there ' and further on, ' I hope to find very few Fools in England on my Return thither, if there remains any considerable number after that immense number We send abroad, We have more Fools then any other nation upon Earth' (Hanbury-Williams MSS, CHW 67 -10929, ff.203-05, The Lewis Walpole Library, Conn.).

Essential Literature: Neilson 1954, no pagination; Sutton 1956, pp.115-16; Russell 1975, pp.115-16.

Fig. 21 after *Reynolds, Mr Turner, Sir William Lowther, Mr Leeson and Mr Huet, oil on canvas,* The Trustees of the Bowood Collection

Fig. 22 Sir Joshua Reynolds, John Woodyeare, Revd Dr Drake, Mr Cook and Charles Turner, *oil on canvas, Museum of Art, Rhode Island School of Design*

Fig. 23 Colonnade at Russborough

the Statues in the Colonnades at Russborough

Chris Caffrey

The twelve classically inspired statues in the niches of the colonnades of Russborough, happily, still perform their original function of declaring to the outside world that the building is a repository of art. The curved Doric colonnades with their full compliment of statues are unique in Ireland (fig. 23).

The most mysterious aspect of the statues' enigmatic history is the fact that they have survived, largely intact, the vagaries of political and cultural change. During the 1798 Rebellion, the house was successfully defended by the Wicklow insurgents, in a running battle on the front lawn, against fellow insurgents from Wexford who intended the complete destruction of the house.[1]

In the 1930s, when the house was owned by Captain Denis Daly, the statues were once again threatened. Captain Daly had eighteenth-century restored antique Roman statues (probably situated in the niches at the rear of the house) removed and dumped after a Sunday sermon by the local parish priest in the church at Ballymore Eustace.[2]

Because of the dearth of accounts and other documentary evidence relating to Russborough, it cannot be said with absolute certainty that the statues were acquired by Joseph Leeson (1711?-1783), 1st Earl of Milltown. There is, however, a considerable body of circumstantial evidence which would seem to indicate that it was indeed the 1st Earl who was responsible for their acquisition. An exhaustive trawl of travel books on Ireland published in the eighteenth century revealed very little. Few mention Russborough and those publications which do usually refer to the house in a cursory manner. None refer to the statues in the colonnades.

It is not until the early nineteenth century that it would seem that any reference to the statues appears in print. Revd. G.N. Wright's *Tours in Ireland etc.* printed in London in 1823 and illustrated with engravings after drawings by George Petrie (1790-1866), seems to be the earliest reference to the statues:[3]

The House, which is built entirely of cut stone, is considered one of the most noble residences in the kingdom; it consists of a centre block, connected with wings by colonnades of the Ionic order [they are in fact Doric], behind which, in twelve niches, stand statues of the heathen divinities. In those on the left are *Jupiter, Ceres, Hercules, Bacchus, Venus* and *Saturn*; on the right *Diana, a Dancing Faun, Tragedy, Comedy, Mercury* and *Apollo*.[4]

There can be no doubt that Wright was describing the copies of antique statues which still remain in the colonnades at Russborough. Essentially he names the statues correctly with only two exceptions; the *Jupiter* which is in fact the *Belvedere Antinous* and the *Apollo* which is the *Apollino*. Wright names the statues in the order in which they are positioned in the colonnades, therefore the statues were acquired and placed there prior to Wright's publication in 1823.[5]

The alignment of the statues in the colonnades demonstrates a coherent ordered sequence. With the exceptions of the *Antinous* in the first niche of the west colonnade and the *Apollino* in the last niche of the east colonnade, the statues are aligned to the central doorways which lead into the quadrant corridors. The effect, more or less, is that the gaze of the statues is set to engage the viewer from both sides as the viewer exits from the quadrant doorways. The doorway of the west colonnade is framed by two male figures, the *Farnese Hercules* and the *Bacchus*, while the doorway of the east colonnade is framed by two female figures, the *Farnese Flora* as the *Muse of Tragedy* and the *Muse of Comedy*.

Iconographically, the two muses relate to the theatre and it is known by the letter from Richard Marley, dated 16 April 1752, to Lord Charlemont in Rome, that Joseph Leeson, 1st Earl of Milltown, had more than a passing interest in amateur dramatics:

'The "Fair Penitent" is to be acted in town by some ladies and gentlemen. Leeson is to play Lothario They say he will do it very ill'.[6]

It is highly probable that the mask held in the right hand of the *Muse of Comedy* is the likeness of Joseph Leeson, 1st Earl of Milltown (fig. 38).

A further humorous touch is displayed in the gender rhythm of the placement of the statues in the niches. If we take male as A and female as B, the rhythm of the statues, starting with the *Belvedere Antinous* in the west colonnade and ending with the *Apollino* in the east colonnade, the sequence is as follows:

A, B, A, A, B, A
B, A, B, B, A, C

Fig. 24 Left colonnade, detail

Fig. 25 Left colonnade, detail

Fig. 26 Right colonnade, detail

Fig. 27 Right colonnade, detail

The startling C is the adolescent god *Apollino* which exudes an androgynous quality (fig. 40).

All the figures are executed in the same type of marble. There is a consistent uniformity and high quality to the handling and finish of the statues which would suggest that they were all produced in the same workshop. The bases of the statues in the west colonnade all reveal the same rough tooled finish, while all the bases of the statues in the east colonnade have the same smooth finish.

Two of the statues are signed with the initials 'B.S': the *Mercury* (fig. 39), which is signed on the exposed surface of the sawn-off branch on the left of the supporting tree stump; and the *Muse of Tragedy* (fig. 37) is signed on the top of the supporting tree stump which rises behind the drapery held

69

by her right hand. Remarkably, only one statue is signed with the sculptor's full name: the *Dancing Faun* (fig. 36) is signed BARTOLOMEO SOLARI F. CARRARA. The signature is on the side hidden from view of the scabellum, a clicking instrument, under the *Faun's* right foot.

Fig. 28 The Dancing Faun, detail showing signature of B. Solari

Bartolomeo Solari (often written as Solaro) was born in Carrara[7] on 22 April 1709.[8] No complete study of the artist has been carried out in Italy to date, and information about him and his work has proved very difficult to find as many documents relating to the eighteenth century have been dispersed or destroyed. Nevertheless, Musetti maintains that it is probable that Solari lived in Genoa between 1729 and 1739 where, according to Lazzoni, 'his sculptures were admired.'[9]

Although currently no documents exist to confirm it, such a hypothesis appears to be backed up by the large presence of sculptors from Carrara who arrived in Genoa in the first half of the eighteenth century, such as Domenico Olivieri, Carlo Cacciatori and Giacomo Antonio Ponsanelli. They entered the workshops of Genovese sculptors and were granted full entry to the Guild of Sculptors and Marble-workers.[10] They showed themselves to have absorbed the teaching of Filippo Parodi (1630-1702) who, elaborating on the work of the Roman school of Pierre Puget (1620-1694), had created a Baroque style and indeed a Rococo style, typically Genovese - precocious and original.[11]

Attributed to this period are four 'quite valuable' bas-reliefs representing the theological virtues and a statue of *Justice*, executed by Solari for the church of S. Rocco in Carrara.[12] He also executed a life-size *Daphne* group for the palace of Count Carlo del Medico, which was later transferred to the vicinity of the Imperial Gallery of the Hermitage.[13]

In 1739, Solari and fellow Carraran sculptor, Giovanni Domenico Olivieri (1708-1762), moved to Turin.[14] They attended the Royal School of Sculpture under the directorship of Simone Martinez (died after 1763), the nephew of the architect royal, Filippo Juvara (1678-1736).[15] The school of sculpture had been founded in 1737 by Charles Emanuel III (1701-1773), 17th Duke of Savoy and King of Sardinia, for his great projects including the enhancement of the city of Turin and the restoration of the Royal Palace. The artistic program of the Royal Court and the presence of numerous academies in Turin made the city an obligatory stopping-point for those on the Grand Tour.[16]

In 1748, Solari finally went to Rome as a result of an annuity given by the King to his most promising artists. Solari was accompanied by the sculptor Ignazio Collino (1724-1793),[17] who was later to succeed Simone Martinez as Director of the School of Sculpture in Turin.[18]

Solari returned to Turin the following year. He executed two colossal statues of *Hope* and *Charity* and the four large crowned angels of the *baldacchino* for the altar of the Sanctuary of Vicaforte near Mondoví.[19] Malle describes the two colossal statues as 'attuned to a substratum of the Roman Bernini culture already tending towards the academic, with stronger overtones of the Tuscan school, finding inflections of elegance and grace charged with an artificial intellectualism which, in certain traits, provokes analogies with the solutions of the minor French Baroque. The quality of the work is very high, and its refined classicism mitigates a certain redundance and irresolution.'[20]

Of the same high quality are two copies of marble *putti* executed by Solari *ca*.1750 for the altars of the church of the Misericordia at Mondoví.[21]

Solari became progressively blind and was forced to abandon his profession. By 1756 he had returned to Carrara and dedicated himself to the apprenticeship of his son Stefano, also a sculptor of talent. No exact date for Solari's death has so far come to light.[22]

Solari was part of the artistic milieu that surrounded the court of Charles Emanuel III. His sculpture comes out of the Late Baroque classical tradition of northern Italy, fostered by Puget and the Roman school through Filippo Parodi in Genoa and reinforced by the pervasive influence of Filippo Juvara in Turin.

The high quality of finish of the statues in the colonnades at Russborough would seem to suggest that they were executed after 1749 when Solari had returned to Turin from Rome. The sophisticated delineation and sheer theatricality of the statues in the niches of the colonnades is the work of a master sculptor at the height of his powers.

Joseph Leeson, later the 1st Earl of Milltown, undertook two Grand Tours, the first from 1744 to 1745 and the second from 1750 to 1751, during which he amassed works of art for Russborough.[23] All of the sculpture which Leeson had acquired on his first Grand Tour and had transported aboard the *Augustus Caesar* was seized by the French at sea early in 1745.[24] It is, therefore, more than probable that Joseph Leeson commissioned the statues from Solari while on his second Grand Tour. It cannot be discounted that Leeson visited Turin. His son, Joseph Leeson (1730-1801), later the 2nd Earl, accompanied him on the Tour and studied at the Royal Academy, Turin.[25]

The statues in the colonnades at Russborough form an integral part of the facade, and the iconographical profile of the statues fits a connoisseur of Joseph Leeson's standing and ambition.

1. A circumstantial account furnished by Geraldine Evelyn, Countess of Milltown, and drawn up by Edward Nugent, 6th Earl of Milltown, in the GSR, vol. 5, p.69.
2. Siggins 1989.
3. J.P. Neale produced two series of pamphlets between 1823 and 1826, *Views of the Seats of Noblemen and Gentlemen in the United Kingdom*. Russborough appeared in the second series in 1826 with an illustration after Neale which shows the niches without the statues (the illustration was reprinted in the Irish Heritage Series: 13, Russborough). The empty niches in Neale's illustration led to the assumption that the statues were nineteenth century copies.
4. Wright 1823, p.149.
5. The Earl of Milltown at the time of Wright 1823 was Joseph Leeson (1799-1866), 4th Earl of Milltown. He had succeeded to the title in 1807 shortly after his eight birthday. His father had died in 1800 before he could succeed to the earldom. The 4th Earl's mother, Emily, remarried in 1811 to Valentine Lawless (1773-1853), 2nd Lord Cloncurry. Joseph was raised from then onwards at Lyons House, Co. Kildare. See Fitzpatrick 1849, p.254.
6. See pp.7-8, note 24.
7. I am deeply indebted to Dr Barbara Musetti, a researcher with Bologna University specialising in eighteenth and nineteenth-century Italian sculptors from Carrara who undertook to research all available publications and extant documents in Carrara referring to Solari on my behalf, and to Michael Berry for his translations.
8. Duomo di S. Andrea, Carrara, Archivio Storico, *Liber Baptismalis Literae ab Anno 1701 usque ad Annum 1725*, p.54.
9. Lazzoni 1880, p.368.
10. In correspondance with Dr Musetti.
11. Nava Cellini 1982.
12. Lazzoni 1880, *loc. cit.*; Thieme-Becker, vol. 31, p. 226. Dr Musetti adds that the church, now de-consecrated, is currently used as a warehouse and all trace of Solari's work has been lost.
13. Dr Musetti has contacted Dr Sergej Androssov who is in charge of the sculpture section of the Hermitage Museum and he hopes before long to be able to find the present location of the work.
14. Tarraga Baldo 1992, vol. 11, p.186.
15. Campori 1873, p.215; Lazzoni 1880, *loc. cit.*; Thieme-Becker, vol. 24, 1907, p.175.
16. Robert Oresko, 'Savoy', in Turner 1996, vol. 28, p.17*ff*.
17. Rovere 1880, p.45.
18. Thieme-Becker, vol. 24, 1907, *loc. cit.*.
19. Theime-Becker, vol. 31, 1907, *loc. cit.*; Malle 1974, p.130; Nava Cellini 1982, p.219.
20. Malle 1974, *loc. cit.*.
21. Bessone 1873, p.14; Malle 1974, *loc. cit.*.
22. Campori 1873, *loc. cit.* states '... but on becoming blind he [Solari] had ceased working and died soon after'; Solari's son Stefano is recorded at the construction of the Royal Palace in Madrid in the second half of the eighteenth century. He was accompanied the his father's friend Olivieri see Tarraga Baldo 1992, vol. 11, pp.185-86.
23. See S. Benedetti's essay, 'The Milltowns'.
24. See p. 7, note 16.
25. Figgis 1994, p.166; see also no. 8, especially note 3.

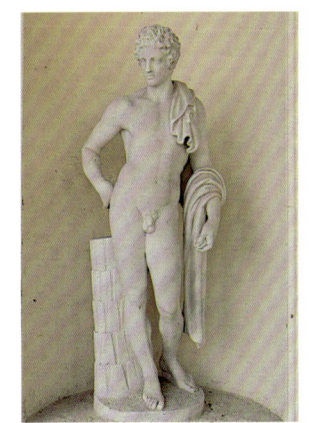

Fig. 29

Belvedere Antinous
Height   1m 65.5cm
Base   5.5 cm. Oval shape, tooled finish.
Damage   to the big toe of right foot.
Original Belvedere Courtyard, Musei Vaticani, Rome

Fig. 30

Ceres
Height   1m 67cm
Base   7 cm. Irregular shape, tooled finish
Original source unknown

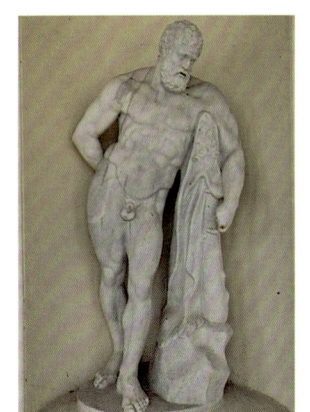

Fig. 31

Hercules
Height   1m 68 cm.
Base   4cm. Large circular shape, tooled finish.
Damage   Thumb and three digits missing from the left hand. Damage to the nose and genitals.
Original in the eighteenth century, in the courtyard of the Palazzo Farnese; now in the Museo Nazionale, Naples.

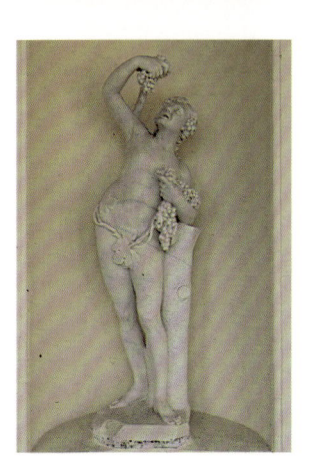

Fig. 32

Bacchus
Height   1 m 79 cm
Base   10.5 cm. Irregular shape, tooled finish.
Damage   to the grapes, to the left hand and the left side of the head
Original source unknown

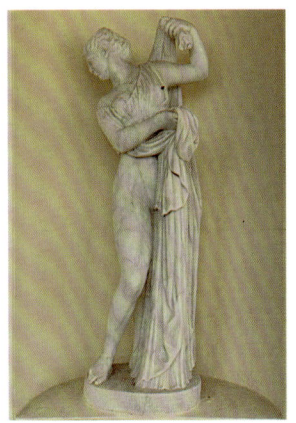

Fig. 33

Callipygian Venus
Height   1 m 61.5 cm
Base   9.5 cm. Oval shape, tooled finish.
Damage   to the tip of the nose.
Original   in the eighteenth century, in the Sala dei Filosifi (surrounded by eighteen ancient sages), Palazzo Farnese; now in the Museo Nazionale, Naples.

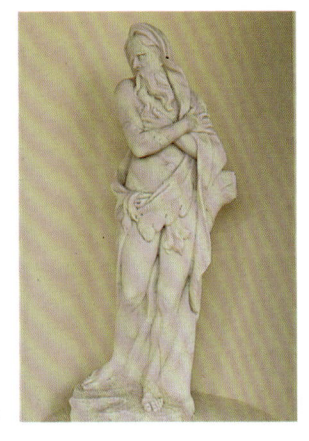

Fig. 34

Saturn
Height   1 m 65 cm
Base   10.5 cm. Irregular shape, tooled finish.
Original   source unknown.

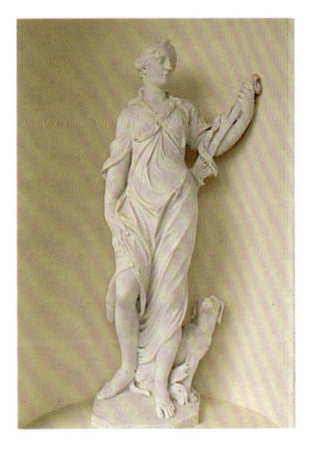

Fig. 35

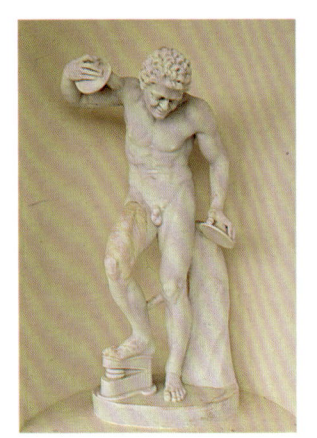

Diana
Height   1m 67 cm
Base   4 cm. Irregular shape, smooth finish.
Original   source unknown.

Fig. 36

Dancing Faun
Signed   BARTOLOMEO SOLARI F. CARRARA on the scabellum under the faun's right foot.
Height   1 m 36.5 cm
Base   9 cm. Oval shape, smooth finish.
Damage   to the thumb and index finger of the right hand. Slight damage to the nose and the chin. The little finger of the left hand and knuckle of the next finger are missing. Damage to the big toe of the right foot.
Original   since the eighteenth century, in the Tribuna of the Uffizi Palace, Florence.

Fig. 37

Farnese Flora
Signed	*B.S.* on the top of the supporting stump.
Height	1 m 59.5 cm
Base	2.5 cm. Irregular shape, smooth finish.
Damage	to the nose.
Original	in the eighteenth century, in the courtyard of the Palazzo Farnese; now in the Museo Nazionale, Naples.

Fig. 38

Muse of Comedy
Height	1m 60 cm
Base	7.5 cm. Oval shape, smooth finish.
Damage	to the nose and slight damage to the mask.
Original	source unknown.

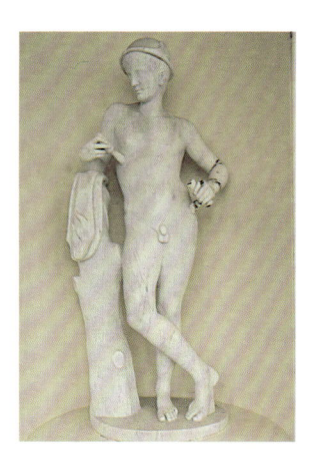

Fig. 39

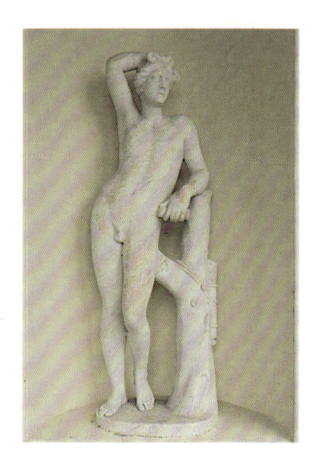

Mercury
Signed	*B.S.* on the exposed supporting stump.
Height	1 m 67 cm
Base	5.5 cm. Oval shape, smooth finish.
Original	since the eighteenth century, in the Uffizi Palace, Florence.

Fig. 40

Apollino
Height	1 m 67 cm
Base	6 cm. Oval shape, smooth finish.
Original	in the eighteenth century, in the Villa Medici, Rome; now in the Tribuna of the Uffizi Palace, Florence.

the **Taste**

PIETRO BELLONI (1695-1771)

24 *Scagliola Console Table-top, 1750*

Inlaid selenite coloured plaster composition, 107 x 211.5 cm

Signed and dated on the lower left corner: *D : Petr.o Belloni Monach:o V:æ F: Anno. Dñi 1750*

Alfred Beit Foundation, Russborough

Provenance: Earls of Milltown (unnumbered, Deed of Gift)

This work is not in the exhibition as it is too fragile to transport.

Don Enrico Hugford, a Vallombrosan Benedectine of the Monastery of Santa Reparata at Marradi near Florence, and elder brother of the painter Ignazio Hugford, was a remarkable craftsman who refined the uncommon art of scagliola composition.[1] This technique, which appears to have started in Emilia in the second half of the sixteenth century as a substitute for real marble, consisted of plaster made with pulverised selenite, mixed with glue and colour.[2]

When Hugford in 1743 became Abbot of Vallombrosa, the principal monastery of his Order, one of his pupils was another monk named Don Pietro Belloni. A small number of signed table-tops realised by him in scagliola are known, and the earliest appears to be the present one, which was one of a pair ordered by Joseph Leeson from Belloni while on his first trip to Italy in 1744-45, during which it is conceivable that he went to Florence.[3] It took a long time for the monk to finish this work and 1750 should be regarded as the completion date.[4]

It is not clear if a second scagliola table-top was ever delivered to Leeson. On the contrary, there is a strong possibility that the monk never made it although Belloni certainly produced a pair for some of Leeson's friends.[5] A pair were made for Ralph Howard of Shelton Abbey, Co. Wicklow and another for Sir Matthew Fetherstonhaugh of Uppark in Sussex.[6]

In each of these, the general design and the decorative motifs used by Belloni are similar. In the centre of the Russborough table a large landscape enclosed in a sort of cartouche is represented against a black background where numerous butterflies are freely rendered. Along the borders, scrolling ribbons richly decorated with flowers are inlaid, interspersed here and there with small animals.[7] At the corners are shell-crowned medallions with pastoral scenes each of which is treated differently with tiny figures in the foreground.

The central landscape shows a river view with boats, fishermen, and a curiously shaped castle in the background. The inspiration for this kind of scene was undoubtedly the work of contemporary painters, like Locatelli, or the Florentine Giuseppe Zocchi who Belloni must have known.

At the time of the gift of the Milltown collection to the National Gallery of Ireland, only the present table-top was recorded and no mention has ever been found of its pendant. After the death of Geraldine Countess of Milltown, in 1914, the console table with this scagliola top was left by the Gallery authorities on loan to the new owners of Russborough and subsequently forgotten.[8] In 1952 when Sir Alfred and Lady Beit purchased the estate, Sir Alfred found and recovered the table-

24

top from a basement. Unfortunately the original Rococo console, now substituted by a neoclassical type, was lost but it must have been as beautiful as the top since it was described, 'in an Old Italian Carved and Gilt Frame of Rich Designs of Scrolls on Foliage and Birds'.[9]

1   Fleming 1955, pp.106-10; Neumann 1959, pp.116-26; Sala and Tarani 1929, vol. I, pp.56-57.

2   Fleming 1955, pp.106-07; Lanzi, 1809, vol. I, p.280, vol. IV, pp.56-59.

3   Coleridge 1966, pp.185-86. In a letter dated 11 July 1747, Horace Mann wrote to Horace Walpole: 'and so slow in working that he [Belloni] has been almost three years about a pair for Mr. Leeson, and requires still six months more '(Walpole Correspondence, vol. XIX (1955), p.423).

4   Cynthia O'Connor instead prefers 1750 as the date of commencement of the work (1980, p.142).

5   In a letter addressed to Sir Horace Mann, at Florence, by Sir Matthew Fetherstonhaugh, after his return to England (1752), he asked the British diplomat to: 'Inquire of the Monk whether he has not done the two tables, of wch kind Mr Leeson had one done', State Papers Foreign, PRO, correspondence of British representatives in Italy, letters to Horace Mann in Florence 1748-72, 105/310, f.161.

6   See Coleridge 1966, pp.185-86; O'Connor 1980, pp.139-42; Jackson-Stops 1985, pp.253-54, no.172.
    From the correspondence between Ralph Howard and Dr James Tyrrell, it appears that Robert Clements also commissioned a pair of tables from Belloni (whereabouts unknown), (letter dated 20 July 1753, Wicklow Papers MSS, NLI).

7   The signature is inscribed on a yellow scroll, on the lower left and, regrettably, it has been reported incorrectly in previous publications. The full latin inscription reads as follows: *Domino Petro Belloni Monacho Vallombrosae Fecit Anno Domini 1750* (fig. 3).

8   Russborough was inherited by Edmund R. Turton, a relative of the last Countess of Milltown. In 1931, the property was acquired by Captain Denis Daly of Dunsandle, Co. Galway.

9   Deed of Gift of The Milltown Collection, 30 June 1902, p.18. From the list of the contents of Russborough hand-written by Geraldine Countess of Milltown, the console table appears to have been kept in the Music Room.

Essential Literature: Fleming 1955, pp.106-10; Coleridge 1966, pp.185-86.

ROSALBA CARRIERA and workshop (1675-1758)

Four Female Portraits, ca.1740

25 *Diana*

Pastel on paper, 35 x 28 cm

26 *Venus*

Pastel on paper, 35 x 28 cm

27 *Autumn*

Pastel on paper, 34 x 26.7 cm

28 *Winter*

Pastel on paper, 34.5 x 28 cm

The National Gallery Ireland (inv. nos. 3844, 3845, 3848, 3849)

Provenance: Earls of Milltown (all four listed under no. 178, Deed of Gift)

The fame of Rosalba Carriera as a portrait pastelist grew considerably in the early eighteenth century when her studio in Venice became a common rendezvous for the wealthiest members of the European aristocracy visiting the city. She started as a miniaturist in the studio of Antonio Balestra but with the encouragement of Christian Cole, an English diplomat, dilettante artist and her great admirer, Rosalba gradually became confident in executing larger scale portraits with crayons.

Cole was also responsible for Rosalba's election as a member of the artists' Academy of St Luke in Rome and for promoting her talent among the British travellers touring in Italy.[1] For these patrons, she started the series of portraits representing the beauties of Venetian high society, which were so successfully received that it became necessary for her sister Giovanna to assist her in producing copies. In 1718, Carriera, with her brother-in-law Giovanni Antonio Pellegrini, was welcomed in Paris and honoured by Crozat, Mariette, Coypel and Watteau, and she was accepted as a member of the local Academy from which women were traditionally excluded.

After her return to Venice, with her eyesight now failing, the artist finally abandoned miniatures and concentrated principally on pastel portraits, for which commissions never ceased until the end of her career.

Although undocumented, we can hypothesise that it was during his first Grand Tour (1744-45) that Joseph Leeson, later first Lord Milltown, purchased his pastels by Rosalba. In addition to the four presented here, there are two more representing the allegorical images of the two remaining seasons, *Spring* and *Summer*.[2] We have no record of a trip to Venice by him at any stage, but given

25

26

the importance of the city he must surely have called there during at least one of his two tours. We know, however, that Robert Wood, who acted as Leeson's secretary, had his portrait made by Rosalba and that in 1742 he purchased a number of female portraits from her including a Diana and one of the Princess Trivulzi.[3] Wood could have acted as agent for Leeson, as he later did in the case of Vernet's seascapes. Alternatively, they could have been ordered on Leeson's behalf by Dr John Clephane, another of his acquaintances during his first tour, who in 1744 was negotiating a set of Rosalba's *Seasons* on behalf of James Dawkins.[4]

It is likely that Leeson's works were executed in the same period and we must accept the possibility that, since Rosalba was losing her sight, she would have been assisted either by Angioletta Sartori or by her sister Angela.

In 1826 when Neale published his survey of the works of art in Russborough, he only reported the four *Seasons*, hanging in the Small Dining Room, and omitted to mention the two goddesses.[5] Like the majority of the paintings in the collection, however, it is possible that their location was never changed and when Geraldine Countess of Milltown wrote her list of the artistic contents of the house, she described the two portraits in the Music Room and confirmed the *Seasons* in the Small Dining Room.[6]

1 Ingamells 1997, pp.227-28.
2 NGI inv. nos. 3846 and 3847.
3 Sani 1988, p.31.
4 Ingamells 1997, p.215.
5 Neale 1826, vol. 3, no pagination.
6 Geraldine Evelyn Leeson Countess of Milltown, hand-written list of works of art in Russborough, dateable to the end of the nineteenth century, (Milltown Papers, NGI Archive).

Essential Literature : Malamani 1910; Sani 1988.

27

28

GIOVANNI BATTISTA BUSIRI, called 'IL TITTA' (1698-1757)

Four Roman Views, ca.1750

29 Landscape with the Tomb of Cecilia Metella

Gouache on paper, 22.9 x 34.5 cm

30 Landscape with a Castle and a Bridge

Gouache on paper, 22.5 x 34.6 cm

31 The Temple of Vesta, Tivoli

Gouache on paper, 22.9 x 34.4 cm

32 The Colosseum

Gouache on paper, 22.6 x 34.5 cm
Signed: *Giō B: sta*

Earls of Milltown (inv. nos. 7400, 7403, 7404, 7405)

Provenance: Earls of Milltown (all four listed under no. 353; they were included with another four in the Deed of Gift, but with no description of the subjects: nos. 149, 151, 152, 153)

As a painter of Roman views, Giovanni Battista Busiri belongs to the tradition of the classical ideal landscape. Vast, open blue skies are the common background for his compositions where vegetation, buildings and figures are flooded by radiant sunshine. His antecedents are clearly traceable in the works of Dughet and van Bloemen, but also in some of his most gifted contemporaries, like van Wittel or van Lint.

What distinguishes Busiri's genre is the commercial production of his works in gouache. Their reduced scale made them more portable and facilitated their sale to foreign visitors.[1]

His tempera landscapes on paper could hardly be called realistic even when they represent well known Roman scenes of the city or the Campagna. Artificially constructed in the studio, making repeated use of early landscape engravings, these pictures were completed with the careful insertion of non-existent ruins. Alternatively, he would paint views of the surroundings of Rome in an Arcadian mood, integrating most of the famous monuments into completely imaginary settings. Nevertheless, in spite of their disputable artistic value, these gouaches were well received by the Grand Tourists who purchased them as souvenirs of what they wanted to believe Rome to be.

Joseph Leeson Senior bought a total of eight small landscapes from Busiri, probably during his second Grand Tour.[2] Three of them were soon copied on a larger scale on canvas by George Barret, to decorate the walls of Russborough.[3]

29

30

Of the four presented here, the first two are of the kind described above, ideal views of the Roman Campagna, with the inclusion of ancient buildings extracted from a different context. In one, the tomb of Cecilia Metella is represented, blended into a rocky landscape. The second shows a river interrupted by several small waterfalls, while in the background a massive castle is reminiscent of the Castello Orsini-Odescalchi in the town of Bracciano, with a picturesque bridge below.[4] The two remaining views, *The Colosseum* and *The Temple of Vesta at Tivoli* are 'realistic', with the addition of a few fictional details.[5]

1. L. Stainton in Wilton and Bignamini 1996, p.153.
2. Ralph Howard, of Shelton Abbey, Co. Wicklow, a neighbour of Leeson, also purchased eight views from Busiri (see Wynne 1996[2], p.462). Howard was in Rome in 1752, and in his purchases of works of art, he widely imitated those made by his friend Leeson. Michael Wynne prefers 1744-45 for Leeson's acquisitions of the gouaches *(ibidem)*.
3. *Ibidem*.
4. This view was thought by Michael Wynne to represent the 'Lake of Bracciano with the Orsini Castle' *(ibidem)*, but as I said it is purely a pastiche.
5. The remaining four Busiris which once belonged to the Earls of Milltown and now in the National Gallery of Ireland are as follows: *The Temple of Minerva Medica* (inv. no. 7401), *The Pantheon* (inv. no. 7402), *The Roman Forum* (inv. no. 7406), and *The Sepulchre of the Plauzi* (inv. no. 7407).

Essential Literature: Busiri Vici 1966; Wynne 1996[2], pp.460-67.

31

32

CLAUDE-JOSEPH VERNET (1714-1789)

The Four Times of Day, 1750

33 Morning ~ Coast scene with Fishermen pulling in their Nets to Shore

Oil on canvas, 104 x 120 cm

34 Midday ~ Rescuing a Ship during a Storm

Oil on canvas, 106.5 x 121.5 cm

35 Sunset ~ Harbour Scene with unloading of Boats

Oil on canvas, 106 x 121.5 cm

36 Night ~ Moonlight with Fishermen setting the Nets

Oil on canvas, 105.5 x 121.5 cm

All signed and dated: *Joseph Vernet f. Romæ 1750*

Alfred Beit Foundation, Russborough

Provenance: Earls of Milltown, by descent to Lady Turton, sold *ca.*1922; Lewis & Simmons, Paris; Private Collection, USA; purchased by Sir Alfred Beit on the art market.

Vernet arrived in Rome in 1734 with letters of recommendation to several French personalities in that city. With the support of those linked to the Papal Court, he was soon comfortably established in the best Roman circles. Although not an official *pensionnaire*, the Director Nicolas Vleughels allowed him to frequent the French Academy and encouraged him to pursue his studies of marine scenes. At the Academy Vernet had the opportunity to attend Panini's lessons on perspective and from him, he learned his technique of soft and atmospheric brushwork. He was also considerably influenced by seventeenth-century painters like Claude Lorrain and, in particular, Agostino Tassi, whose coastal scenes were at the time still visible in many Roman palaces. Among his favourite subjects, the Neapolitan coastline was the principal source of inspiration for Vernet.

In 1745, he married Virginia Parker, the daughter of an Irishman enrolled in the Papal Navy. In the same year he painted his first sets of marine scenes, capturing the light at four different stages of the day, for British Grand Tourists.[1]

Joseph Leeson at that time preferred to commission from him a copy of *The Death of Atilius Regulus*, a canvas painted one century earlier by Salvator Rosa (no. 41). The idea of having a set of seascapes must have occurred to him some time after his return to Ireland. Russborough was not completed until about 1748 and the interior work, including stuccoes and furnishings, must have taken further time. Leeson, on the point of departing for his second tour, must have decided to decorate a drawing room with Vernet's pictures. Certainly the choice of paintings with an oval

33

34

shape was dictated by the style of plasterwork which was being carried out on the walls of his house.[2] We have no proof that the future Earl of Milltown was in Rome when the commission for the four coastal scenes was ordered from Vernet. Actually, it is documented that it was Robert Wood, not yet famous for his discoveries, who in December 1749 ordered these four landscapes from Vernet on behalf of Joseph Leeson. From the artist's *livre de raison* (account book) we learn that he promised to deliver the finished canvases for the middle of 1751 for the sum of 300 Roman ducats.[3] And it is interesting to note, from the requested date of completion of the pictures, that Leeson had already decided to extend his Roman sojourn.[4]

At the time the French artist had a studio and apartment in the Palazzo Zuccari. Thomas Patch, who resided in the same building at the time was apprenticed to Vernet.[5] Undoubtedly, Irish and British connoisseurs were frequently invited to visit this atelier, and there they found these marine pictures so captivating as to induce them to order several sets from Vernet.[6] Not all these commitments were honoured, but among those tourists who were able to return with a series of 'four times of the day' marine scenes by Vernet was Joseph Henry.[7]

1 In January came the commission from James Dawkins (1722-1757) and in February from William Drake (1723-1796).
2 The plasterwork in Russborough is one of the most important Rococo undertakings of the Ticinesi brothers Lafranchini in Ireland. It may reasonably be presumed that the wall decoration of the Drawing Room in Russborough, including the stucco frames of the Vernets, was reasonably made after the arrival of the pictures in Ireland. The paintings were never conceived as overdoors as has been proposed (see Laing 1995, p.214, note 11).
3 Lagrange 1864, *Livre de Verité*, p.331, no.93, *Reçus*, p.360, no.38.
4 As I said before, Joseph Leeson most probably returned to Ireland for the end of 1751.
5 Vernet lived in Palazzo Zuccari from 1748-53. For Patch see Watson 1939-1940, p.17.
6 In the *Livre de Vérité* (Lagrange 1864) these names are listed: John Bouverie, Benjamin Lethieullier, Sir William Lowther, Sir Matthew Fetherstonhaugh, Thomas Dawson, pp.331-35.
7 The current location of these pictures is unknown, but a *Coast scene with Castle and Figures* by Vernet (lot. 366) was auctioned on 19 October 1937 by Jackson Stops & McCabe, at Straffan House, Co. Kildare.

Essential Literature: Neale 1826, no pagination; Lagrange 1864 p. 331, 360; Ingersoll Smouse 1926, p.59; Conisbee 1976, p.11, nos. 25-28, no pagination.

35

36

GIOVANNI PAOLO PANINI (1691-1765)

Four Landscapes, 1742

37 Landscape with The Colosseum and the Arch of Costantine

Oil on canvas, 72.5 x 98 cm

38 The Roman Forum

Oil on canvas, 72.5 x 98 cm

39 A Capriccio with St Paul preaching to the Romans with the Temple of Vesta and the Pyramid of Cajus Cestius

Oil on canvas, 72.5 x 98 cm

40 A Capriccio with St Peter preaching to the Romans

Oil on canvas, 72.5 x 98 cm

All signed: *I.P. Panini Romæ 1742*

National Gallery of Ireland (inv. nos. 725, 726, 727, 728)

Provenance: Earls of Milltown (nos. 326, 205, 206, Deed of Gift)

Panini left his native Piacenza and reached Rome in 1711. There he worked first as an assistant to the excellent painter Benedetto Luti and, once independently settled in 1719, he was admitted into the Academy of St Luke. From the 1720s his descriptive compositions of the Eternal City became well known among collectors and foreign visitors and due to continuous demand Panini frequently replicated his landscapes, although with minor variations.

These four landscapes were purchased by Joseph Leeson during his first visit to the Rome. He did not commission recognisable views from the artist but preferred to choose canvases from Panini's most typical and renowned production, two topographical scenes of famous ancient sites and two *Capricci*. This last genre in particular allowed Panini the freedom to create timeless images of a world were people lived unaffected by the surrounding ruins of their glorious past.

Equally successful were his more traditional, realistic compositions, but even in their 'reality', Panini always liked to add some small element which did not belong to the original scene. For instance in our view of the Colosseum, the statue of the Borghese Gladiator (at the time still in the famous Villa) is included on the left, or in the canvas which shows the Roman Forum with the unexpected presence on the right of a large classical crater (which belonged to the same collection).[1]

As we know, the canvases are dated 1742 which raises the question of when Leeson purchased

37

38

them.[2] Well, we also know that he is not recorded in Italy before 1744 and so, unless we consider the possibility that his journey was initiated much earlier, which seems unlikely, we should consider that the future Earl of Milltown bought landscapes which were already available from a Roman agent or more plausibly from the artist himself. One of the *cognoscenti* met by Joseph Lesson in Italy was Dr John Clephane, a Jacobite 'bear leader' who had been in that country before and who frequently acted as well as an agent in transactions of *objets d'art*.[3] He knew Panini since 1742 when he made a payment to him for paintings ordered two years earlier by Lord Mansell. He was in Rome again in 1744 and could have been instrumental in the acquisition of these four views. On one occasion at least, we are aware of Leeson placing a commission with him. This was in October of 1744 in Rome when, during a dinner with other gentlemen, he asked Clephane to purchase for him a 'Dresden snuff box'.[4]

1 Arisi 1961, pp.162-63, nos.137-38.
2 Wynne 1986, pp.83-84 incorrectly dates them 1740. Of the same date, 1742, are two *Capricci* in the Musée de Grenoble (MG 28-29) one of which is in many ways similar to our no. 39 (see Chiarini 1988, pp.80-82).
3 M. Wynne in Ingamells 1987, p.593.
4 F. Russell in *Ibidem*, p.215

Essential Literature: Arisi 1961, pp.162-63, 167-68, nos. 137, 138, 153, 154; Wynne 1986, pp.83-84; Arisi 1993.

39

40

CLAUDE-JOSEPH VERNET (1714-1789)

41 *The Death of Atilius Regulus*

Oil on canvas, 155 x 224 cm

National Gallery of Ireland (inv. no. 1045)

Provenance: Earls of Milltown, (no. 169, Deed of Gift)

The scene represents a celebrated episode in the history of the Roman Republic. The Consul, Marcus Atilius Regulus was captured during a battle and sent by the Carthaginians to Rome to persuade the Senate to accept their peace conditions. Instead, Atilius Regulus convinced his countrymen to continue the war and, having given his word that if the Romans refused he would return to Carthage to be judged, he loyally returned to his enemy who sealed him up in a barrel driven through with spikes.

Salvator Rosa, who painted the original version of this dramatic subject around 1652, wanted to exalt the stoicism of the hero, and in the eighteenth century his picture was considered one of the most famous paintings in Rome.[1] When Joseph Leeson commissioned this copy in March 1745 from Vernet, Rosa's canvas was in the collection of the Colonna Princes in their Palazzo beside the Church of SS. Apostoli, and it could be seen and admired by every Grand Tourist.[2] As a result, the copy is accurate to the original in every respect including the dimensions which are practically the same.[3]

It may seem curious that a wealthy man like Leeson, certainly one of the richest tourists ever in Rome, would choose to commission copies when he could afford to purchase originals but, at the time, it was considered quite proper to acquire copies of well-known pictures or sculptures for one's home. After all, permission could rarely be obtained for the export of famous works out of Rome.[4]

1 Salerno 1963, pp.97-99, 121-22, no. 33; Wallace 1967, pp.395-97.
2 Colonna Catalogue 1783, no. 206.
3 In his *Livre de raison*, Joseph Vernet described: '31. Pour M. Lisson [sic] *Anglois une copie d'une tableau de Salvator Rosa qui est dans la gallerie Collonna* [sic], *representent Attilius Regulus, de même grandeur de l'original, a cents écû ordonné au mois de mars de l'an 1745, promis pour le mois de may de la meme année*' (in Lagrange 1864, p.324). The original is now in the Virginia Museum of Fine Arts, Richmond, and its dimensions are 152 x 216 cm.
4 According to Neale's survey of 1826 the Vernet copy was hanging in the Saloon while in the hand-written list by the Countess of Milltown at the end of the nineteenth century (NGI Archive) it is in the Dining Room of Russborough.

Essential Literature: Wynne 1971.

41

GIOVANNI BATTISTA PIAMONTINI (fl.1725-1762)

42 Arrotino (The Knife Sharpener)

White marble 70 x 83.7 x 37.7 cm

43 The Wrestlers

White marble 71 x 74 x 46.5 cm

Both inscribed on the pedestal: *IOANNES PIAMONTINIUS/SCULP: FLORENT: MDCCLIV*

National Gallery of Ireland (inv. nos. 8210, 8211)

Provenance: Earls of Milltown (no. 251, Deed of Gift)

Innumerable copies were made after the originals of these two sculptures. The *Arrotino* (Knife-grinder), as this marble was commonly called by the end of the seventeenth century, was an unidentified subject for a long time. Antiquarians made several different suggestions - a Roman slave whetting his knife, a barber who had spied the conspiracy of Catiline, and many others. The solution came from the observation of a gem carved with the myth of Apollo and Marsyas in which this figure was represented as the Scythian executioner, waiting for God's orders. This solution is now widely accepted and it is also agreed that the statue is probably an authentic Pergamene marble.[1]

The *Wrestlers* appears to share the same origin, Pergamon, although it is clear that a bronze sculpture was the archetype for it.[2] The fame of both statues was at its height during the eighteenth century and at that time they were exhibited in the Uffizi Tribuna, an obligatory place to visit for any gentleman who wished to acquire good taste.[3]

The artist who made these copies, Giovanni Battista Piamontini, was the son of the more renowned sculptor, Giuseppe Piamontini.[4] His name was probably suggested to Joseph Leeson by Dr James Tyrrell.[5] He was an artist capable of producing original work although his activity has not yet been fully investigated. As a copyist, he must have been one of the best in Florence as he was reputed as 'remarkable for being a slave to the originals'.[6]

---

1 See Haskell and Penny 1981, pp.155-57, no.11.
2 *Ibidem*, pp.337-39, no.94.
3 The most emblematic image of the Tribuna is Zoffany's famous painting in the Royal Collection.
4 Born in Florence (1664-1742), pupil of Giovanni Battista Foggini, his works are in several churches in Florence.
5 Dr Tyrrell acted as agent in Florence for Leeson dispatching paintings to him (see O'Connor 1980, p.136).
6 This was said by Tyrrell, referring to some busts commissioned from G.B. Piamontini by Ralph Howard (letter of Dr Tyrrell to Ralph Howard, 7 September 1752, Wicklow Papers, NLI).

42

43

ANTONIO JOLI (ca.1700-1777)

44 *Embarkation of the King of Spain at Aranjuez, ca.1750*

Oil on canvas, 76 x 129.5 cm

Signed: *Imbarco di piacere di S.M.[C.] in Ara[njuez] Joli 17...*

Private Collection

Provenance: Henry of Straffan, Co. Kildare; purchased in Sinclair's (art dealers), Nassau Street, Dublin, by the father of the current owner

Antonio Joli is not only one of the most distinguished Italian landscape painters of the eighteenth century, but also one of the most itinerant. After an early apprenticeship in his birthplace, Modena, he moved to Rome where he practised as a painter of theatrical scenes in the workshops of several prominent artists, like Panini. In 1735 in Venice he came into contact with Canaletto. Enriched by that experience, and alternating his activity as a painter of stage sets with that of easel painter, he visited first Germany and, in 1744, London where he stayed for four years. From 1750 to 1754 he was in Madrid after which he returned to Venice where he became a founding member of the Venetian Academy. Finally, his artistic ability was fully acknowledged when he obtained the position of court painter in Naples, first to Charles VII and, when he left to become King of Spain, to his son Ferdinand I, ending his career there.[1]

This view shows the famous Royal Palace of Aranjuez, favourite residence of King Philip V, the first Bourbon Spanish monarch, who had the building reconstructed in a Baroque style and the gardens enlarged to emulate those of his grandfather Louis XIV at Versailles. In the centre the King and Queen aboard the Royal boat are saluted by the crowd as they depart for a pleasure trip along the river Tagus.

Although there is no direct evidence, it is probable that this picture originally belonged to Joseph Henry. Richard Twiss, who visited Straffan before 1775, reported that Henry owned several landscapes by Joli, all painted in 1750. According to the writer, the scenes represented a bullfight, and views of Naples, Madrid and Aranjuez.[2] The date of 1750 corresponds with the beginning of Joli's sojourn in Spain and, from a different source, it is known that Joseph Henry went to that country during the autumn of 1752.[3]

As a collector of paintings, Henry shared the same taste as his uncle Joseph Leeson. He owned canvases painted by Batoni, Reynolds and Vernet and liked the seventeenth-century Florentine artists. Like Ralph Howard, he had landscapes by Wilson,[4] and a copy of Raphael's *Madonna della Seggiola* made in pastel by the English painter Charles Martin[5] but perhaps the picture which he took most pride in was a life size *Madonna* painted by Carlo Dolci, and described as a masterpiece.[6]

44

1 Lanzi 1809, vol. IV, pp.55-56; The Golden Age 1981, vol. I, pp.119-21.
2 Twiss 1775, p.27.
3 'Our friend Henry passed the summer at Marseilles being afraid of the heats of Spain, but he set out for that country last week', letter of James Tyrrell to Ralph Howard, Florence 8 October 1752, Wicklow Papers, NLI. This information was found and published by Cynthia O'Connor in 1980, p.139.
4 The two landscapes painted by Wilson in Rome in 1752 and owned by Henry were sold at Foster's on 25 May 1870. Purchased by Barbara, Countess of Milltown they became part of the Milltown Collection and were gifted to the National Gallery of Ireland in 1902 (inv. nos. 746 and 747). This information was provided by Ellis Waterhouse: see Wynne 1974, p.110. The difficulty in tracing a copy of the Foster's sale catalogue made it impossible for this author to verify if other paintings belonging to Henry were also on sale at the same time.
5 Twiss 1775, pp.26-27.
6 It appears to have originaly been painted for Filippo Franceschi, and was recorded in 1775 in *Elogio di Carlo Dolci* (Baldassari 1995 p.36, note 1) as acquired by the Irish *'Giuseppe Henery'* [sic]. Francesca Baldassari has suggested that the painting represents a *Virgin in Glory*, now at Stanford University (inv. no. 79.103; 117 x 97 cm) see Baldassari 1995, pp.161-62. An oil painting of a *Madonna and Child*, allegedly by Carlo Dolci, was included in the Straffan House Sale, on 20 October 1937 (Jackson Stops & McCabe's sale catalogue, Straffan House, Co. Kildare, 18/25 October 1937, p.37, lot 736).

workshop of PIER LEONE GHEZZI (1674-1755)

45 *Portrait of Pope Benedict XIII*

Oil on canvas, 56.5 x 49.8 cm (fragment)

National Gallery of Ireland (inv. no. 1084)

Provenance: Earls of Milltown

The son and grandson of painters, Pier Leone Ghezzi is today best remembered as a caricaturist, but he was a musician and antiquarian and, most of all, he was a polyhedric artist capable of producing different genres of painting. As a painter of historical canvases his most important official commission was for six large scenes from the life of Pope Clement XI for the papal palace of Castelgandolfo while for the Prince Falconieri he produced decorative frescoes in different residences. He also painted landscapes views, but it was in the genre of portraiture that he became most famous.

He produced innumerable portraits using various media throughout his life. His models were mainly members of the Papal Court or artist-colleagues from the Academy of St Luke, or from the foreign community in Rome with whom, particularly the French, he maintained strong contacts. He also painted the portrait of Pope Clement XI for which he was highly praised.[1] In the *Lives of Popes and Cardinals from Clement X to Clement XII*, published by Mario Guarnacci in 1751, Ghezzi contributed numerous drawings of decorative motifs and portraits, leaving them to other artists to engrave.[2] Among those portraits there is one of Benedict XIII just at the beginning of the description of his Papacy, which is said to be have been drawn by Ghezzi after his oil portrait (fig. 41).[3] Although the sources are silent regarding this, we cannot exclude the possibility that this Pope was indeed portrayed by the artist.

It is evident that the present, fragmentary, canvas was copied after the engraving or after another oil painting very similar to it. Even though its quality is not very high, it is useful to demonstrate the sort of connection that Joseph Leeson may have had with Ghezzi's studio. Moreover, the fact that a Protestant visitor bought a portrait of a Pope should not surprise us. It is well known that by and large Grand Tourists maintained excellent relations with the Catholic hierarchy in Rome and, because they were attracted by the temporal power of the Popes, many desired (and succeeded), to be received by the 'Successor of St. Peter' during private audiences.[4]

1 Pio. Ms. 1977, p.154.
2 Guarnacci 1751, p.409.
3 *Eques Petrus Leo Ghezzius delin, et pinx / Hieronymus Rossi incid./ Domenicus de Rossi Hoeres Io. Iacobi formis Romæ ad Templ. S. M. de Pace cum Priv. S. Pont.*
4 There was a '*Dispensation to Joseph, 1st Earl of Milltown, from Pope Benedict XIV*' in the Library at Russborough but we do not know what it was obtained for because the document is, regrettably, lost.

45

*Fig. 41 Engraving from Guarnacci 1751,
Author's Collection*

BARTOLOMEO CAVACEPPI (?1716-1799)

46 *Faun with a Kid*

White marble, 69 cm high

47 *Faun with a Goat*

White marble, 75 cm high

Both sculptures are inscribed on the pedestals: BARTOLOMEUS CAVACEPPI SCÛLP RÔM 1751

National Gallery of Ireland (inv. nos. 8243, 8242)

Provenance: Earls of Milltown (no. ?261, Deed of Gift)

Like many artists in Rome at the time Bartolomeo Cavaceppi was also an antiquarian and dealer, but it is as a restorer of antique sculpture that he became particularly renowned, having renovated most of Cardinal Albani's collection after it was purchased by Pope Clement XII in 1733 and displayed in the new Capitoline Museum. Cavaceppi was continuously approached by Italian and foreign agents who were interested in selling 'pristine' sculptures to Grand Tourists, the original parts of which were frequently minimal.[1]

Another lucrative business for Cavaceppi was the replication of antiques in various sizes and media. The two marble copies presented here were acquired by Joseph Leeson during his second trip to Rome as is clear from their inscriptions. Regrettably, we have no documents to establish whether these works were directly commissioned by the Irishman or were already available in the artist's studio. It is possible that Leeson came into contact with Cavaceppi through the 'small' architect, Mattew Brettingham, who knew and had traded with the sculptor since 1749.[2]

The first of the two sculptures is a reduced copy of the famous *Faun with the Kid*, a Roman marble of the second century AD which was found in 1676 near the Chiesa Nuova in Rome and, having been in the collections of Queen Christine of Sweden and of the Prince Odescalchi, it was acquired by Philip V and brought to Spain in 1724.[3] The fact that the sculpture was no longer in Rome did not diminish its reputation nor impede its reproduction. A plaster cast was known to be in the French Academy as a model for the students and Cavaceppi would have had easy access to that.[4]

The second Faun was also a copy of a Roman statue of the second century AD. This was discovered in 1736 in Hadrian's Villa at Tivoli and then transferred to the Capitoline Museum where it was constantly admired by visitors during the eighteenth century for its particular dark-red marble.[5] Cavaceppi knew this second sculpture so well that he later copied it again and this time in life size.[6]

As we can judge, both of Leeson's marble copies were executed in a highly skilful manner by the artist and they must have been considered by the later Earl of Milltown as among his best souvenirs from Italy.[7]

46

47

1   Howard 1982.
2   J. Kenworthy-Browne (entry on Matthew Brettingham) in Ingamells 1997, pp.122-23.
3   The sculpture is now in the Prado Museum (height 136 cm) see Blanco y Manuel Lorente 1969, pp.24-25.
4   Haskell and Penny 1981, pp. 211-12, no.37.
5   *Ibidem*, pp.213-15, no.39.
6   Cavaceppi 1768-72, vol. I, plate 28.
7   At the end of the nineteenth century the two sculptures were displayed in the Small Drawing Room of Russborough (Geraldine Countess of Milltown, hand-written list, NGI Archive).

48 *Roman Cinerary Urn*

White marble, no lid, 26 x 45 x 31 cm

Inscribed: D • M• S / L• CALTILI •/ SALVTARIS / CALTILIA • POLITICE / ET • SABINVS • LIB / P • B •M • F

49 *Roman Cinerary Urn*

White marble, no lid, 43 x 37.3 x 27.3 cm

Inscribed: D M / PHILOCALO C • S / VLPIA • ATTICLIA / CONIUGIE MF

National Gallery of Ireland (nos. 8288, 8279)

Provenance: The Earls of Milltown (no. 265, Deed of Gift)

ROMAN 18TH CENTURY *after the antique*

50 *Portrait Bust of Seneca*

White marble with grey marble socle, 59 cm high

National Gallery of Ireland (inv. no. 8276)

Provenance: Earls of Milltown (no. 264, Deed of Gift)

Among the *objets d'art* and souvenirs purchased in Italy by the Earls of Milltown there were a very limited number of original antiques. In the inventories we find reference to a few statues, unfortunately no longer traceable, and to some busts and to three cinerary urns. Of the three pieces shown here only the two urns are authentic while the bust is definitely a late copy. The so-called *Seneca* was for centuries one of the most sought after sculptures. The stoic philosopher was considered a rare example of morality and, like the busts portraying other great men of the past, replicas of it were frequently purchased to adorn libraries in accordance with a legend that Cicero had his own decorated in the same way.[1] Significantly, this fashion was thus explained by Dr James Tyrrell: '… to inspire good morals and Patriotisme to certain Bucks who begin to prefer *amor pecunia*, to the inestimable *amor Patria*'.[2]

The two urns are instead original Roman marbles and were acquired, together with a third, by Joseph Leeson, later 1st Earl of Milltown. Their purchase was made in 1751 according to an important source,[3] and confirmed by a document which until now has not been fully considered.[4]

Both urns are very elegantly decorated. In the first a frieze is carved alternating *bucrania* with festoons of foliage. The second is much more elaborate, in the shape of a tabernacle with palms, festoons and small animals. Above there is a garland with the head of Medusa in the centre while below the dedicatory inscription the door of the kingdom of Hades is symbolically represented.

48

49

1 See Venuti 1783, pp.11-19; Haskell and Penny 1981, p.52.

2 Wicklow Papers, letter of Dr James Tyrrell to Ralph Howard, Florence 7 September 1752, NLI. Ralph Howard, through the agency of James Tyrrell, commissioned two busts of Tully and Seneca from Piamontini for his uncle Lord Chief Justice Henry Singleton. Unfortunately, it appears that the marbles arrived damaged in Ireland because they were badly packed (see O'Connor 1980, p.139).

3 The inscription of no. 48 is recorded in the *Corpus Inscriptionum Latinarum*, vol. VI, no. 14257 with a note attributed to Count Aurelio Guarneri Ottoni that it went to England in 1751. An identical note in the same Corpus (vol. VI, no. 36099), referring to Ridolfino Venuti, concerns no. 49. See Purser 1925, Appendix, pp.31-32.

4 On 10 June 1751 James Russell exported from Rome four tables, two renovated heads and three marble urns. See Bertolotti 1878, p.213. This document should refer to antiques destined for Joseph Leeson since all are reasonably identified in the Milltown inventories. This request of export by James Russell is also mentioned, with the incorrect date of 1758, in Ingamells 1997, p.832.

50

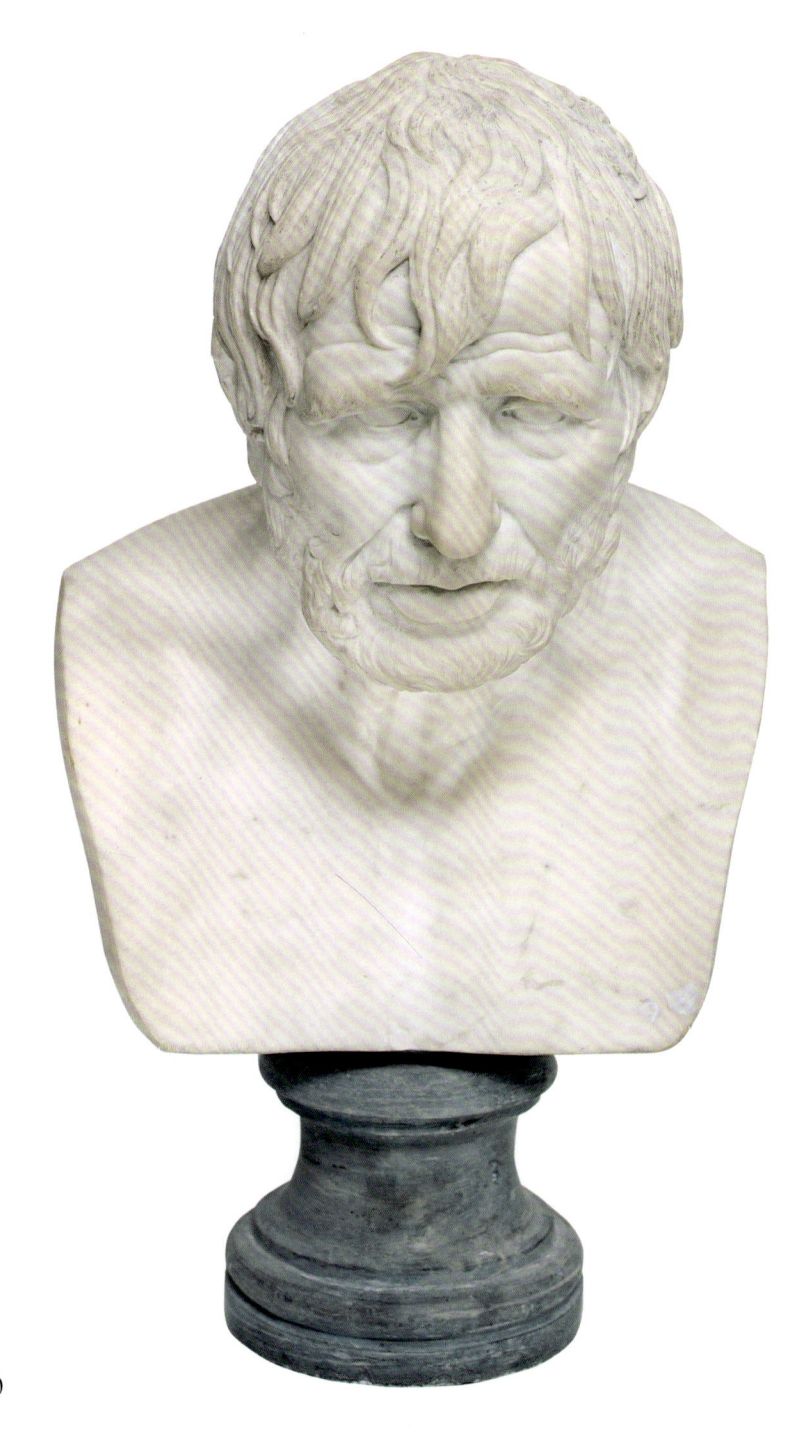

workshop of FERDINANDO TACCA (1619-1686) after models by GIAMBOLOGNA (1529-1608)

Four Labours of Hercules

51 Hercules clubbing the Lernaean Hydra

Bronze statuette, 41 cm high

52 Hercules and the Erymanthian Boar

Bronze statuette, 45 cm high

53 Hercules slaying the Nemean Lion

Bronze statuette, 31.8 cm high

54 Hercules with the Pillars

Bronze statuette, 33.5 cm high

National Gallery of Ireland (inv. nos. 8121, 8123, 8124, 8125)

Provenance: Earls of Milltown (nos. 77, 79, 83, 85, Deed of Gift)

Some time before 1581, Giambologna made a set of small sculptures on the theme of the *Twelve Labours of Hercules* for Francesco I de' Medici, Grand Duke of Tuscany. It is not sure what material they were made in but we know that, between 1576 and 1589, silver casts were obtained from six of these models for display in the Tribuna of the Uffizi.[1] With the exception of one of Giambologna's wax-models,[2] neither his originals nor the silver casts still exist. The reconstruction of the *Twelve Labours* is, therefore, largely based on bronze copies made after him by his pupils.

His favourite assistant Pietro Tacca (1577-1640) inherited his studio (which included the many models left there), and he also succeeded his master as court sculptor. Tacca made several bronzes of the *Labours* at the request of the Grand Duke, one set of which was apparently destined for James I of England in 1612.[3] In turn his son Ferdinando became Granducal sculptor and inherited the workshop in Borgo Pinti, in Florence.

Ferdinando is known to have cast and sold statues from Giambologna's original models. Today, just a few, mostly incomplete, sets of the *Labours* are accounted for.[4] The four bronzes presented here were certainly purchased in Florence by the 1st or the 2nd Earl of Milltown. The first two *Hercules*, with the *Hydra*, and with the *Erymanthian Boar*, are generally recognised as being from Giambologna's models.[5] The remaining two, *Hercules with the Nemean Lion* and *Hercules with the Pillars* reflect the style of the master, but should be attributed to a follower. The *Hercules with the Pillars*, it should be said, is not strictly speaking a 'Labour' of the mythical hero, and we cannot even be sure if this subject would have figured in the original set made by Giambologna.[6]

51

52

The handling of all of these four bronzes - the patina, heavy casting, lack of chiselling, and broad modelling of the heads - indicates that they were produced by the same artist. Furthermore, as has been noted, some of the details of execution are typical of Ferdinando Tacca, the last artist to produce the sophisticated mannerism of Giambologna.

It is not certain if originally these sculptures were a complete set or if there were others included. There are at least two pairs of small bronzes in other collections which have strong similarities with them, but this matter has not yet been fully investigated.[7]

1 Radcliffe 1978[1], p.12.
2 *Ibidem*, p. 16.
3 Radcliffe 1978[2], p.122.
4 Eleven groups of sculptures thus exist, see Radcliffe 1978[1], p.16.
5 Radcliffe 1972.
6 *Ibidem*.
7 *Ibidem*. There are two bronzes formerly in the Salomon Collection and now whereabouts unknown, and two in the Wallace Collection, London: *Hercules overcoming Antæus* (S.120), and *Hercules and the Arcadian Stag* (S.123). See Mann 1931, pp.45-47, pl.34.

53 54

GAETANO GALLELLA, Italian second half 18th century

55 *Fan with a Bacchanal*

Mother-of-pearl fan with nineteen sticks, the sticks and guards carved, pierced, gilt and silver appliqués, painted, length 26 cm, span 47.5 cm

Signed on the lower right: *Gae / Gallella*

National Gallery of Ireland (inv. no. 12042)

Provenance: Earls of Milltown (no. 123, Deed of Gift)

The use and making of fans was widespread all over Europe in the eighteenth century. Topographical images of the most important cities and classical subjects were the prerogative of the Italian production. Famous paintings by the most celebrated artists like Raphael and Guido Reni were also widely used. On this fan the scene represented is apparently a 'Bacchanal'. At the centre is Silenus, portrayed as a fat, jolly, old man. Kneeling in front of him with grapes in her hand, is a Bacchante, while behind, two satyrs of different ages are carrying and pouring wine into the cup of the god. On the left are two more female figures one of whom is lying on the ground from the after-effects of the wine. On the far right a group of young people is feasting near a fountain. Practically all the figures here are copied from the ceiling painted by Pietro da Cortona in the Palazzo Barberini in Rome. On the verso of the fan where, as usual, a much less important subject is painted, there is a classical ruin which appears to be the so called *Arco oscuro*, a picturesque ancient arch located near Villa Giulia, in Rome.[1] The front of the sticks also show a classical theme, the *Triumph of Galatea*.

1 Colini 1966, nos. 1-4, pp. 14-21.

55

55 verso

ANONYMOUS, French 18th century

56 *Fan with a Fête Champêtre*

Ivory fan with twenty-two sticks, sticks and guards carved, pierced, painted and gilded, length 29 cm, span 56 cm

National Gallery of Ireland (inv. no. 12043)

Provenance: Earls of Milltown (no. 126, Deed of Gift)

Many French painters like Watteau, Lancret and Pater, provided compositions for fans in the eighteenth century. Although the scene reproduced on the front of this fan cannot be attributed to any one of those artists, it is painted in their spirit and style. A group of young people, apparently travellers, amuse themselves observing the skill of one of their party, jousting what seems to be his pilgrim stick. Seated on the right is an hurdy-gurdy player, probably waiting for his turn to perform. On the verso a simple subject is painted, a young boy picking flowers from a plant. On the lower side of the front the sticks are decorated alternately with fluted ionic pilasters and colourful Rococo scrolls.

56

56 verso

Fig. 42 Irish ca. 1750, Chinoiserie mirror, detail, National Gallery of Ireland

Russborough -
its decoration and furniture, some preliminary thoughts
The Knight of Glin

Joseph Leeson, later Lord Russborough and Earl of Milltown, the connoisseur son of a Dublin brewer and unscrupulous property developer decried by Swift, succeeded to his considerable family fortunes in 1741 after his father died.[1] A year later he bought a service of high rococo plate by the London Silversmith George Wickes - a foretaste of his considerable interest in the decorative as well as the fine arts.[2]

Leeson bought the lands of Russborough in 1741 and began to plan his great Palladian complex there to the designs of the German born architect Richard Castle who is said to have collaborated with Francis Bindon. In 1744-45 and in 1750-51 he was on the Grand Tour in Italy spending huge sums on pictures and antique sculpture for his new house. This was 'forming into perfection' by 1748[3] and Castle was dead by 1751 so Bindon may have completed it.

Fig. 43 Detail of the Saloon ceiling at Russborough

The plaster work is superb and one of the Lafranchini brothers executed the Saloon ceiling, where the putti representing the four seasons and further putti playing in the scroll work of the cove (fig. 43) are echoed in the carving of the heads of those decorating the three mirrors. It seems not unlikely that the pair of great pier glasses (no. 58) hung on either side of the Corinthian columned pedimented mahogany door case which leads into the hall. The landscape mirror (no. 59) possibly surmounted the superb marble chimney piece by Thomas Carter the younger imported from London (fig. 44). Another landscape mirror now in the hall of the National Gallery house No. 90 Merrion Square could have decorated the west wall.[4] A number of floral decorated oval mirrors also from Russborough survive and a pair of these could have hung between the windows facing the garden front (fig. 45).[5] Paintings would have made up the rest of the hanging.

Richard Castle had his own favourite band of craftsmen and early he used John Houghton (fl.1729-1761) in partnership with John Kelly (fl.1739-1773) for carving both in stone and wood. The tympanum of the pediment at Carton is documented as being executed by them in 1739 and the superlative architectural wood carving at Tyrone House, Clanwilliam House, Leinster House and, I believe, at Russborough is possibly attributable to their workshops.[6] The carved Rococo mahogany detail on the overdoors in the hall at Russborough, the capitals of the columns in the Drawing Room and the carved treads of the magnificently crafted staircase all show this superb quality. It therefore seems not unlikely that

Fig. 44 Thomas Carter the younger, marble chimney piece in the Saloon at Russborough

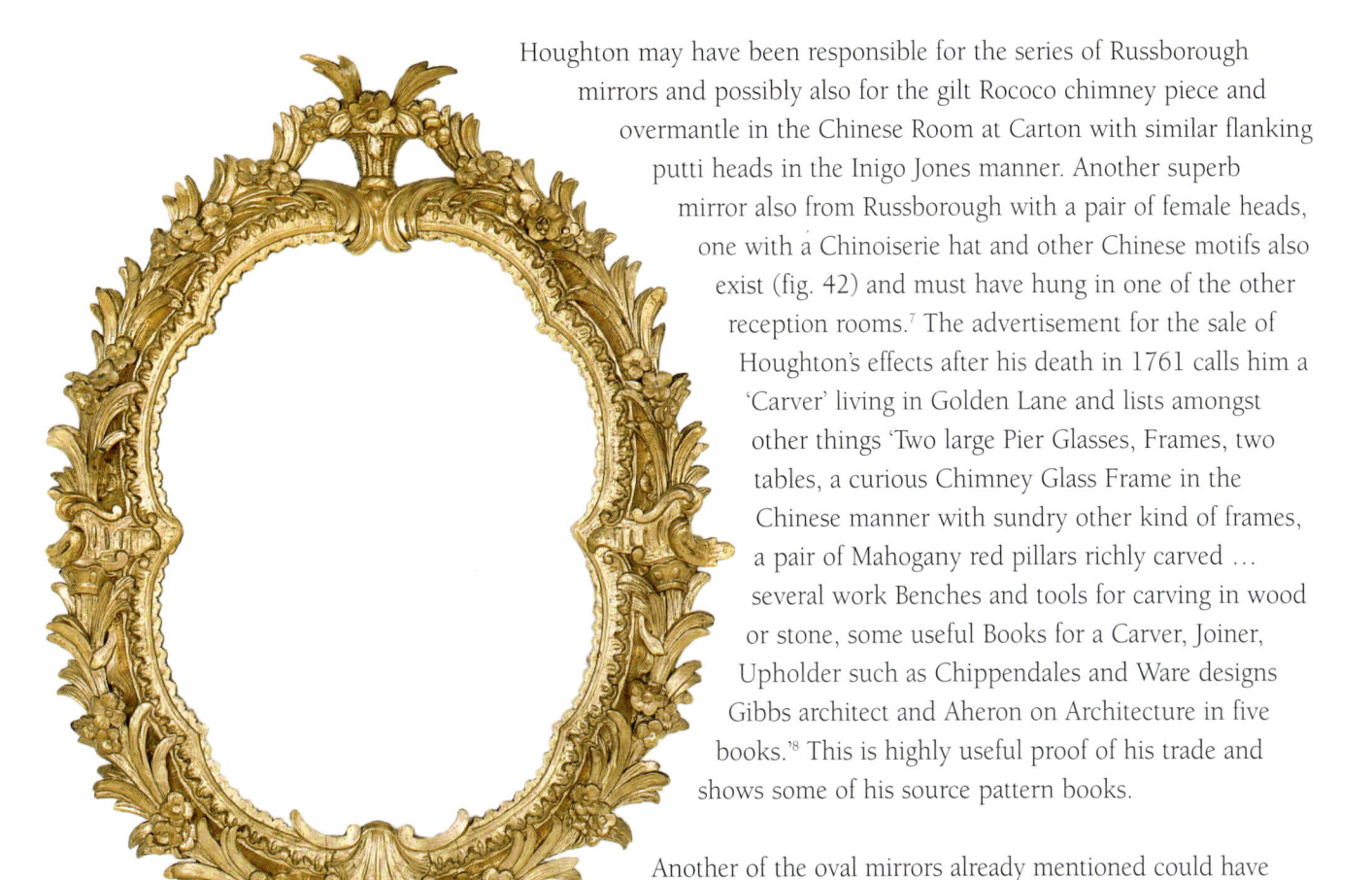

Fig. 45 Irish ca. 1750 Oval mirror, National Gallery of Ireland

Houghton may have been responsible for the series of Russborough mirrors and possibly also for the gilt Rococo chimney piece and overmantle in the Chinese Room at Carton with similar flanking putti heads in the Inigo Jones manner. Another superb mirror also from Russborough with a pair of female heads, one with a Chinoiserie hat and other Chinese motifs also exist (fig. 42) and must have hung in one of the other reception rooms.[7] The advertisement for the sale of Houghton's effects after his death in 1761 calls him a 'Carver' living in Golden Lane and lists amongst other things 'Two large Pier Glasses, Frames, two tables, a curious Chimney Glass Frame in the Chinese manner with sundry other kind of frames, a pair of Mahogany red pillars richly carved … several work Benches and tools for carving in wood or stone, some useful Books for a Carver, Joiner, Upholder such as Chippendales and Ware designs Gibbs architect and Aheron on Architecture in five books.'[8] This is highly useful proof of his trade and shows some of his source pattern books.

Another of the oval mirrors already mentioned could have ideally fitted into the blank plaster cartouche between the windows of the Drawing Room - the other cartouches house the four Vernet paintings (nos. 33-36) and Joseph McDonnell attributes the decoration of this room and the Dining Room to another stuccadore, possibly German who also worked at St Peter's Drogheda in 1752, by which time Russborough must have been almost complete.[9] The outstretched winged eagle surmounting this Drawing Room cartouche and those on the pier glasses combined with the plaster putti in the Drawing Room ceiling suggest a close collaboration between the plasterers and the wood carvers. It is relevant to note that Houghton and Kelly were working at Carton in 1739 significantly at the same time as the Lafranchini were decorating the Saloon there - a further collaboration under the eye of Richard Castle at Russborough seems highly likely.

Turning to the sources of these amazing Russborough mirrors, it is obvious that Houghton and/or Kelly must have known the engraved suites of Mathias Lock. Lock was the pioneer Rococo furniture designer in England before Thomas Chippendale[10] and he must have been inspired by Gravelot who was the chief conduit of the French rocaille style from France to England. Lock's first set of designs appeared between 1740 and 1746. One of them, *Six Sconces*, appeared in 1744 and the eagle and putti decorated asymmetrical mirror is certainly the inspiration for the Russborough pair of pier glasses.[11] Other similarities and comparisons can be traced. The rocaille carved work from Lock and Copeland's *A New Book of Ornaments* appeared in 1752 so his oeuvre is fashionably contemporary for Russborough's furnishing and decoration. Lock's French Rococo inspired hand incorporates heads with Chinese hats, Bacchic masks, animals, birds and acanthus which are all delicately interpreted in the carving of these Russborough mirrors.

Turning to the mahogany tables and noting the long set of seat furniture, we meet with a possible change of craftsman. Houghton or Kelly may not have been responsible for the pair of rather awkwardly attenuated tables with their heavily sculpted aprons (no. 57). A monumental swan pedimented cabinet on stands in the Victoria and Albert Museum may well be by the same Dublin carver.[12] The tables, though robustly carved with fruit, flowers, cabochons and acanthus, composition-wise are a far cry from the sophisticated lines of the mirrors. They were presumably made for the Russborough Dining Room and their grooved superstructure at the back of their tops were utilised to display the salvers and dishes of Leeson's rich service of Wickes Rococo plate, so they really acted as platforms for this magnificent show of silver. These glittering dishes, tureen, etc. would have harmonised well with the Baroque/Rococo transitional ceiling with its shells, urns, acanthus and eagles.

Russborough in its heyday must have been an opulent sight. Lady Kildare notes in 1759 when she paid a visit that 'the house is really fine, and the furniture magnificent, but a frightful place'. This last remark was obviously directed at Mr Leeson rather than the house for she was scandalised by the fact that he was entertaining at the time of her visit a notorious woman named Oliver and her daughter, 'ensconced there playing hostesses'.[13]

By the time the Georgian Society photographed the house in 1913[14] many of the paintings and furniture must have left for the National Gallery under the terms of Lady Milltown's request of 1902. Some of the long set of seat furniture, however, remained there when Sir Edmund Turton Bt., Lord Milltown's nephew, inherited the property.[15] Some of these pieces can be seen in the Georgian Society's rather sad photograph of the hall ranged around the room, the chairs fitting flush with the chair rail. A humped backed sofa and day bed can also be seen. Some of these sofas and day beds are in the National Gallery and in a private collection in Co. Wicklow. They are all upholstered with wine coloured cut velvet, the same material which hangs in the Saloon to this day in the usual eighteenth century convention. This velvet, previously considered early-nineteenth-century, may well date from the 1750s. The set of chairs have square backs and the whole suite has finely carved claw and ball feet and elegantly turned stretchers.

The Russborough mirrors and furnitures are enormously important for understanding the arrangement of mid-eighteenth-century decoration in Ireland. There are no more complete collections of original furnishings in a major house here. For instance, Castletown only has some fine remnants of its original contents, Powerscourt was burned, the Provost House a few items, Malahide likewise, Newbridge was almost intact but over the last few years much has been removed. Carton and Florence Court are also empty of almost all their original pieces - a sad tale indeed. How stimulating it would be to one day carry out an historical exercise in the form of an exhibition at Russborough to return some of the furnishings, paintings and other contents and try to place them in their original positions. This would be a vital lesson for those interested in the history of Ireland's eighteenth-century decorative arts.

1. Laetitia Pilkington relates much libidinous scandel about Leeson and his father's *arriviste* activities. Much shocking information is gathered together in Pilkington 1754, 1997 ed., vol. 1, p.134 and pp.302-03 and footnotes vol. II, p.691.
2. See McDonnell 1997, p.85 illus., pl. 15. This tureen and other pieces of the service are part of the Milltown gift to the NGI in 1902.
3. Quoted in the entry for Russborough in A Tour of Two Gentlemen 1748, reprinted in FitzGerald 1913, p.68.
4. Illustrated in O'Brien with Guinness 1994, p.125.
5. A pair of these are shown in the Drawing Room of Áras an Uachtaráin, *ibidem*, p.115.
6. For the most recent information on Houghton and Kelly see FitzGerald 1997, pp.17-18 and particularly footnotes 10, 11, 15 and 18.
7. Now in the NGI No. 90 Merrion Square. Illustrated in O'Brien with Guinness 1994, p.124.
8. Faulkners Dublin Journal, 9-13 June, 1761: quoted in Guinness 1997, p.20, footnote 18.
9. O'Donnell 1991, pl. 102; for Russborough see pls. 87,88, 100-03 and pp.22-24.
10. See Ward Jackson 1958, pp.13, 14, 38, 40, pls. 48-67; and White 1990 pp.38, 39 and *passim*.
11. Illustrated in Ward Jackson 1958, pl.51. A pair of huge pier glasses with winged eagles and Diana heads, and birds were at Headfort, Co. Meath. Three other superb Rococo mirrors were also there, all inspired by Lock and probably from the same Houghton/Kelly workshop. Another tripartite overmantel mirror with an eagle cresting originally at Donacomper, Co. Kildare, also belongs to this group. For illustrations see the photographic furniture files at Glin Castle, Co. Limerick. For other mirrors by and inspired by Lock see Wills 1965, pls.60-68.
12. Illustrated in Coleridge and FitzGerald 1966, pl.10. Another side board identical to the Russborough pair is at Kilruddery, Co. Wicklow.
13. Leinster Letters, vol. 1, pp.76-77 and Pilkington 1754, vol. 2, p.691.
14. GSR, vol. 5, pl.LVI.
15. Sir Edmund Turton Bt. sold Russborough to Denis Daly in 1931 and many of the chairs remained there in his time. A number have come onto the market since and it was said that there were at least twenty in the set. Four were sold at Christie's, 8 February, 1996, lots 194-95.

IRISH ca.1750

57 *Pair of sidetables*

National Gallery of Ireland (inv. nos. 12,001, 12,002, illus.)

Provenance: Earls of Milltown (unnumbered, Deed of Gift)

A pair of elaborately carved side tables, the aprons composed with acanthus leaves, flowers and cabochons, supported by cabriole legs with square hairy paw feet and bulging acanthus decorated hocks. Both 84 x 250 x 83 cm. (K of G)

57

IRISH *ca.*1750

58 *Pair of Gilt Pier Glasses*

National Gallery of Ireland (inv. nos. 12,003, 12,004, illus.)
Provenance: Earls of Milltown (unnumbered, Deed of Gift)

Pair of gilt pier glasses, the asymmetrical cresting surmounted by an eagle with outstretched wings, the sides composed with scroll work, rocaille decoration, bunches of rushes, acanthus and putti heads, the base centred with a mask of Bacchus. Both 243 x 102 cm. (K of G)

IRISH *ca.*1750

59 *Overmantle*

National Gallery of Ireland (inv. no. 12,158)

Provenance: Earls of Milltown (unnumbered, Deed of Gift)

A landscape shaped overmantle similarly composed with an eagle with thunderbolts, putti heads and a Bacchic mask, 210 x 234 cm. (K of G)

60 *Two handle cup*

Hallmarks: London 1663

Maker: *GD* within a heart shaped shield

Not traced. 24 cm high

National Gallery of Ireland (inv. no.12,208)

Provenance: Earls of Milltown (unnumbered, Deed of Gift)

Vase shaped body is mounted on a circular gadrooned foot, the scroll handles having beaded decoration. The flat lid is enriched with a beautifully modelled finial.

Vast quantities of cups were manufactured throughout the seventeenth and eighteenth centuries. Excessive drinking took place on festive occasions, the chief stimulating agent being the number of toasts proposed in accordance with the fashion of the time. (Douglas Bennett)

60

61 *Chocolate pot*

Hallmarks: London 1710
Maker: Jonathan Newton
26 cm high

National Gallery of Ireland (inv. no.12,210)
Provenance: Earls of Milltown (unnumbered, Deed of Gift)

Plain tapering body, lateral handle, curved spout with hinged cap and high moulded domed lid.

Chocolate was introduced into England about 1650. Hot chocolate was a bitter drink and had to be served piping hot. The finial on the lid could be removed and a long tube or muddler was inserted through the lid to mix the drink and stir any chocolate that had sunk to the bottom of the pot, thus preventing loss of heat created by opening the lid. (DB)

61

62 *Punch bowl*

Hallmarks: London 1710

Maker: John Othan Read

26 cm high

National Gallery of Ireland (inv. no.12,209)

Provenance: Earls of Milltown (unnumbered, Deed of Gift)

The bowl with straight fluting. Armorials within scroll work cartouches. Circular stepped base with gadroon decoration. Removable notched top.

Punch bowls were among the most impressive and notable objects in the late-seventeenth and early-eighteenth centuries. Many of them had removable notched tops allegedly to hang glasses. They were named Monteiths after a Scot who lived in Oxford and wore a scalloped gown. (DB)

62

63 Quart tankard

Hallmarks: London 1713
Maker: John Ruslen
20 cm. high

National Gallery of Ireland (inv. no. 12,211)
Provenance: Earls of Milltown (unnumbered, Deed of Gift)

Plain tapering body with central band. Bold scroll handle with ornamental thumb piece. Protruding domed lid extending over rim.

Late-seventeenth and early-eighteenth century tankards were usually capacious and relatively plain. They were used for drinking ale and beer. (DB)

64 *Pair of candlesticks*

Hallmarks: Dublin 1751

Maker: Peter Desenard

20.5 cm high

National Gallery of Ireland (inv. no. 12,212, 12,213)

Provenance: Earls of Milltown (unnumbered, Deed of Gift)

The cast shaped stems having flat chasing and applied husk decoration supported on shaped bases.

The first candlesticks appeared in Ireland after the Restoration and usually had fluted columns and large drip pans. In the eighteenth century the baluster form ousted the columnar candlestick and all sorts of elegant shapes began to emerge. Casting in moulds was fashionable as were stepped bases. (DB)

65 *Pair of candlesticks*

Hallmarks: London 1767

Maker: Emick Romer

35 cm high

National Gallery of Ireland (inv. no. 12,214, 12,315)

Provenance: Earls of Milltown (unnumbered, Deed of Gift)

The fluted columns having acanthus corinthian capitals, the stepped bases with reed and foliate borders.

The fluted column was reintroduced when continental travel was the order of the day and was considered to be one of the essentials of a good education. Excavations at Pompeii and Herculaneum resulted in people undertaking the Grand Tour some of whom did elegant drawings of both Greek and Roman antiquities. (DB)

65

66 *Coffee or hot water jug*

Hallmarks: London 1775
Maker: Andrew Fogelberg
34 cm high

National Gallery of Ireland (inv. no. 12,216)
Provenance: Earls of Milltown (unnumbered, Deed of Gift)

The neo-classical pear shaped body having repoussé work of hanging festoons and rams' heads, beaded borders, high flat handle covered in cane or wicker to act as an insulator.

The Adam or Neoclassical influence was found both in England and Ireland from about 1770. Based on the designs of a young Scottish architect who not only designed buildings but the contents as well. In his own words 'we have been able to seize with some degree of success, the beautiful spirit of antiquity, and to transform it with novelty and variety through all our numerous works'. (DB)

Bibliography

Arisi 1961: F. Arisi, *Gian Paolo Panini*, Piacenza 1961

Arisi 1986: F. Arisi, *Gian Paolo Panini e i fasti della Roma del '700*, Rome 1986

Arisi 1993: F. Arisi, *Giovanni Paolo Panini 1691-1765*, exhib. cat., Palazzo Gotico, Piacenza 1993

A Tour of Two Gentlemen: *A Tour of Two Gentlemen in Ireland*, Dublin 1748

Baldassari 1995: Francesca Baldassari, *Carlo Dolci*, Turin 1995

Baudi di Vesme 1968: C. Baudi di Vesme, *L'arte in Piemonte dal XVI al XVIII secolo*, Turin 1968

Bean and Griswold 1990: J. Bean and W. Griswold, *Eighteenth Century Italian Drawings, in the Metropolitan Museum of Art*, New York 1990

Bellori 1751: G.P. Bellori, *Descrizione delle immagini dipinte da Raffaelle de Urbino, nel Palazzo Vaticano*, Rome 1695, 2nd ed. Rome 1751

Bertolotti 1878: 'Esportazioni di Oggetti di Belle Arti da Roma per l'Inghilterra nei secoli XVII e XVIII', *Archivio Storico Artistico Archeologico e Letterario*, Anno IV, vol. II, fasc. 5, Rome, 1878

Bessone 1873: G. Bessone, *Nuova Guida Storico-Artistica del Santuario di Nostra Signora di Mondoví*, Turin 1873

Black 1992: J. Black, *The British Abroad - The Grand Tour in the Eighteenth Century*, Stroud 1992

Blanco y Manuel Lorente 1969: A. Blanco y Manuel Lorente, *Museo del Prado-Catalogo de la Escultura*, Madrid 1969

Bodart 1976: D. Bodart, 'Pier Leone Ghezzi, the draftsman', *Print Collector*, vol. 7, no. 31, March-April 1976, pp.12-31

Bowron 1980: Edgar Peters Bowron, *A Scholar Collects, Selections from The Anthony Morris Clark Bequest*, exhib. cat., Philadelphia Museum of Art 1980

Bowron 1982: Edgar Peters Bowron, *Pompeo Batoni and his British Patrons*, exhib. cat., Iveagh Bequest, Kenwood House 1982

Burke's Landed Gentry: *Burke's Landed Gentry*, London 1912

Burke's Peerage: Burke, *The Peerage and Baronetage*, London 1890

Busiri Vici 1966: A. Busiri Vici, *Giovanni Battista Busiri, Vedutista romano del '700*, Rome 1966

Campori 1873: G. Campori, *Memorie Biografiche degli Scultori, Architetti e pittori Nativi di Carrara e di Altri Luoghi della Provincia di Massa*, Modena 1873

Cavaceppi 1768-72: B. Cavaceppi, *Raccolta d'antiche statue, busti, teste cognite ed altre sculture antiche*, Rome 1768-72

Charlemont Manuscripts: *Manuscripts and Correspondence of James, First Earl of Charlemont*, Historic Manuscripts Commission Reports, Twelfth Report, X, 1891

Chiarini 1988: Marco Chiarini, *Tableaux italiens: Catalogue raisonné de la collection de peinture italienne XIV-XIX siècles*, Grenoble 1988

Clark 1963: Anthony Morris Clark, 'Pierleone Ghezzi's Portraits', *Paragone*, no. 165, 1963, pp.11-21

Clark 1985: Anthony Morris Clark, *Pompeo Batoni: A Complete Catalogue of his Works with an Introductory Text*, Oxford 1985

Colonna Catalogue: *Catalogo dei Quadri e Pitture esistenti nel Palazzo dell'Eccellentissima Casa Colonna in Roma*, Rome 1783

Coleridge 1966: Anthony Coleridge, 'Don Petro's Table-tops: Scagliola and Grand Tour Clients', *Apollo*, vol. 83, March 1966, pp.184-87

Coleridge and FitzGerald 1966: Anthony Coleridge and Desmond FitzGerald, 'Eighteenth Century Irish Furniture a Provincial Manifestation', *Apollo*, vol. 84, October 1966, pp.276-89

Colini 1966: A.M. Colini, 'L'Arco oscuro', *Bolletino dei Musei Comunali di Roma*, vol. XIII, 1966, pp.14-21

Conisbee 1976: P. Conisbee, *Claude-Joseph Vernet, 1714-1789*, exhib. cat., Kenwood 1976

Cornforth 1963: John Cornforth, 'Russborough, Co. Wicklow', *Country Life*, CXXIV, 5, 12, 19 December, 1963, pp.1464-67; 1623-27; 1686-90

Cotton 1856: W. Cotton, *Sir Joshua Reynolds and his Works*, London 1856

Crookshank 1989-90: A. Crookshank, 'Robert Hunter', *Irish Arts Review Year Book*, 1989-90, pp.169-85

Crookshank and Knight of Glin 1969: A. Crookshank and the Knight of Glin, *Irish Portraits 1660- 1860*, exhib. cat., Dublin 1969

Crookshank and the Knight of Glin 1978: A. Crookshank and the Knight of Glin, *The Painters of Ireland, c.1660-1920*, London 1978

Cust 1914: L.H. Cust, *History of the Society of Dilettanti*, London 1914

DNB 1968: *Dictionary of National Biography*, Oxford 1968

Donald 1996: D. Donald, *The Age of Caricature, Satirical prints in the Reign of George III*, New Haven & London 1996

Earl of Ilchester 1928: The Earl of Ilchester, *The life of Sir Charles Hanbury-Williams*, London 1928

Evans 1956: J. Evans, *The Society of Antiquaries*, London 1956

Figgis 1994: N.F. Figgis, 'Irish Artists, Dealers and Grand Tourists in Italy in the Eighteenth Century', UCD, Unpublished Doctoral Thesis 1994

Finaldi 1997: G. Finaldi, 'Portrait of a lady of The Milltown Family as Shepherdess by P. Batoni', in *Discovering the Italian Baroque: The Denis Mahon Collection*, exhib. cat., National Gallery, London, 1997, pp.30-31

FitzGerald 1913: B. FitzGerald, *Russborough*, The Georgian Society Records of 18th Century Domestic Architecture and Decoration in Dublin, Dublin 1913, vol. 5, pp.68-71, pls. L-LXX, pp.128-29, 232-33

FitzGerald 1937: B. FitzGerald, 'Russborough, Co. Wicklow', *Country Life*, 23 and 30 January, 1937, pp.94-99; 120-26

FitzGerald 1950: B. FitzGerald, *Lady Louisa Connolly, 1743-1821, an Anglo-Irish Biography*, Kent 1950

FitzGerald 1997: Desmond FitzGerald, 'Irish Furniture in Florence Court', *Apollo*, vol. 145, April 1997, pp.16-20

Fitzpatrick 1849: W.J. Fitzpatrick, *Life and Times and Contemporaries of Lord Cloncurry*, Dublin 1849

Fleming 1955: John Fleming, 'The Hugfords of Florence', *The Connoisseur*, November-December 1955, pp.106-10;197-206

Fleming 1957: John Fleming, 'Two rediscovered portraits by Allan Ramsay', *The Connoisseur*, March 1957, p.76

Fleming 1962: John Fleming, *Robert Adam & his Circle in Edinburgh and Rome*, Cambridge, Mass. 1962

Girouard 1958: M.Girouard, 'Alscot Park, Warwickshire -III', *Country Life*, CXXIII, 15, 22, 29 May 1958, pp.1064-67;1124-27;1184-87

Godfrey 1984: R. Godfrey, *English Caricature 1620 to the Present*, Victoria and Albert Museum, 1984

Graves and Cronin 1899: A. Graves and W.V. Cronin, *History of the Works of Sir Joshua Reynolds PRA*, London 1899

GSR: Georgian Society Records, Records of Eighteenth Century Domestic Architecture and Decoration in Ireland, 5 vols., Dublin 1909-1913

Guarnacci 1751: M. Guarnacci, *Vitæ, et res gestæ Pontificum Romanorum et S.R.E. Cardinalium a Clemente X, usque ad Clementem XII*, 2 vols., Rome 1751

Hanbury Williams Papers: Walpole S. Lewis Library, Farmington

Harbison et al. 1978: Peter Harbison, Homan Potterton and Jeanne Sheehy, *Irish Art and Architecture*, London 1978

Haskell and Penny: Francis Haskell and Nicholas Penny, *Taste and the Antique:The Lure of Classical Sculpture 1500- 1900*, New Haven & London, 1981

Howard 1982: Seymour Howard, *Bartolomeo Cavaceppi, Eighteenth-Century Restorer*, New York 1982

Ilchester and Stavordale 1901: Countess of Ilchester and Lord Stavordale, *The Life and Letters of Lady Sarah Lennox: 1745 - 1826*, London 1901

Ingamells 1997: *A Dictionary of British and Irish Travellers in Italy 1701-1800*, compiled by John Ingamells from the Brinsley Ford Archive, London 1997

Ingersoll-Smouse 1926: F. Ingersoll-Smouse, *Joseph Vernet, peintre de marine 1714-1789*, 2 vols., Paris 1926

Jackson-Stops 1985: *The Treasure Houses of Britain: Five Hundred Years of Private Patronage and Art Collecting*, ed. by Gervase Jackson-Stops, exhib. cat., National Gallery of Art, Washington - New Haven & London 1985

Kenworthy-Browne 1983: J. Kenworthy-Browne, 'Matthew Brettingham's Rome Account Book 1747-54', *Walpole Society*, 49, 1983, pp.37-132

Lagrange 1864: L. Lagrange, *Les Vernet, Joseph Vernet et la peinture au XVIIIe siècle*, Paris 1864

Laing 1995: Alastair Laing, In *Trust for the Nation: Paintings from National Trust Houses*, London 1995

Lanzi 1809: L. Lanzi, *Storia Pittorica di Italia*, 3rd edition, 5 vols., Bassano 1809

Lazzoni 1880: C. Lazzoni, *Carrara e le Sue Ville*, Carrara 1880

Leeson 1963: F. Leeson, 'The Milltowns Leesons, A Provisional History of the Family of Leeson Earls of Milltown, in the Peerage of Ireland', 1963, Unpublished Typescript in NGI Library and in the British Library

Leeson Memoirs: *The Memoirs of Mrs Leeson*, 3 vols., Dublin 1795; new edition by M. Lyons, Dublin 1995

Leinster Letters: *Correspondence of Emily, Duchess of Leinster (1731-1814)*, 3 vols., ed. by Brian FitzGerald, 1949, 1953 and 1957

Leppert 1988: R. Leppert, *Music and Image*, Cambridge 1988

Lippincott 1983: L. Lippincott, *Selling art in Georgian London: the rise of Arthur Pond*, New Haven & London 1983

Lo Bianco 1985: Anna Lo Bianco, *Pier Leone Ghezzi*, Palermo 1985

Lodge 1789: J. Lodge, *The Peerage of Ireland*, 7 vols., Dublin 1789

Mahon 1947: Denis Mahon, *Studies in the Seicento Art and Theory*, London 1947

Malamani 1910: V. Malamani, *Rosalba Carriera*, Bergamo 1910

Malone 1798: E. Malone, 'Account of the life ...', in J. Reynolds, *The Work of Sir Joshua Reynolds ...*, 2nd ed., London 1798

Malle 1974: L. Malle, *Le Arti Figurative in Piemonte dal Secolo XV al Secolo XIX*, Turin 1974

Mann 1931: J.G. Mann, *Wallace Collection Catalogue - Sculpture*, London 1931, with supplement 1981

McDonnell 1991: Joseph McDonnell, *Irish Eighteenth Century Stucco Work and its European Sources*, exhib. cat., National Gallery of Ireland, 1991

McDonnell 1997: Joseph McDonnell, 'Irish Rococo Silver', *Irish Arts Review Yearbook*, vol. 13, 1997, pp.78-87

Miller 1982: J. Miller, *The Catalogue of Paintings at Bowood House*, 1982

Morgan 1824: Lady Morgan, *The Life and Times of Salvator Rosa*, 2 vols., London 1824

Morpurgo 1927: E. Morpugo, 'English Physicians-Doctorati-at the University of Padua in 'Collegio Veneta Artista (1616-771)', *Proceedings of the Royal Society of Medicine*, vol. XX, 1927

National Gallery of Ireland 1981: *National Gallery of Ireland Illustrated Summary Catalogue of Paintings*, NGI, Dublin 1981

National Gallery of Ireland 1992: *Master European Paintings from the National Gallery of Ireland*, US touring exhib. cat., NGI, Dublin 1992

Nava Cellini 1982: A. Nava Cellini, 'La Scultura del Settecento', *Storia dell'Arte Italiana*, Turin 1982

Neale 1826: J.P.Neale, *Views of the Seats of Noblemen and Gentlemen in England, Wales, Scotland and Ireland*, 2nd series, 5 vols., London 1826

Negri 1970: Arnoldi F. Negri, 'Il Ritratto di Clemente XI di Pierleone Ghezzi e una sua medaglia dell' Amerani', *Paragone*, no. 239, 1970, pp.67-73

Neumann 1959: E. Neumann, 'Materialen zur Geschichte der Scagliola', *Jahrbuch der Kunsthistorischen Sammlungen in Wien*, vol. XIX, 1959, pp.116-26

Neilson 1954: Katharine B. Neilson, 'A Caricature by Sir Joshua Reynolds', *Museum Notes*, Rhode Island School of Design, Providence, vol. 11, no. 2, Winter 1954

Northcote 1818: J. Northcote, *The Life of Sir Joshua Reynolds*, 2 vols, London 1818 [2nd ed. revised and augmented of 1813-15]

Nygren and Pressly 1977: E.J. Nygren and N.L. Pressly, *The Pursuit of Happiness: a View of Life in Georgian England*, exhib. cat., New Haven, CT, 1977

O'Brien with Guinness 1994: Jaqueline O'Brien with Desmond Guinness, *Dublin: A Grand Tour*, London 1994

O'Connor 1980: Cynthia O'Connor, 'Dr James Tyrrell, agent in Florence', *Irish Studies*, Summer 1980, pp.138-44

O'Connor 1983: Cynthia O'Connor, 'The Parody of the "School of Athens" - The Irish Connection', *Irish Georgian Society*, vol. 26, 1983, pp.5-22

Pascoli 1736: L. Pascoli, *Vite de'Pittori, Scultori, ed Architetti moderni*, 2 vols., Rome 1736

Pasquin 1796: A. Pasquin [John Williams], *Memoirs of the Royal Academicians and Authentic History of the Artists in Ireland*, London 1796, rev. ed. by Lightbown, 1970

Penny 1986: Nicholas Penny, 'An Ambitious Man - The Career and the Achievement of Sir Joshua Reynolds', in *Reynolds*, exhib. cat. by N. Penny et al., Royal Academy of Arts, London 1986

Pilkington 1754: *Memoirs of Laetitia Pilkington*, 1754, new edition in 2 vols. ed. by A.C. Elias Jr, Athens (Ga.) & London 1997

Pio Ms. 1977: Nicola Pio, *Le vite di Pittori Scultori et Architetti*, edited by Catherine and Robert Engass, Città del Vaticano 1977

Purser 1925: L.C. Purser, 'Classical Inscriptions at Shanganagh Castle, Co. Dublin', *Proceedings of the Royal Irish Academy*, Dublin 1925, pp.1-35

Radcliffe 1972: A. Radcliffe, 'Typescript comments on the Four Bronzes', 10 July 1972, NGI Archive

Radcliffe 1978[1]: A. Radcliffe, 'Giambologna's Twelve Labours of Hercules', *The Connoisseur*, September 1978, pp.12-19

Radcliffe 1978[2]: *Giambologna 1529-1608, Sculptor to the Medici*, exhib. cat. ed. by Charles and Anthony Radcliffe, Arts Council of Great Britain 1978

Ribeiro 1983: Aileen Ribeiro, *A Visual History of Costume: The Eighteenth Century*, London 1983

Ribeiro 1984: Aileen Ribeiro, *Dress in eighteenth century Europe 1715-1789*, London 1984

Ribeiro 1995: Aileen Ribeiro, *The Art of Dress, fashion in England and France 1750 to 1820*, Yale 1995

Roëttgen 1993: Steffi Roëttgen, *Anton Raphael Mengs, 1728-1779, and his British Patrons*, exhib. cat., Kenwood 1993

Rovere 1880: C. Rovere, *Descrizione del Real Palazzo di Torino*, Turin 1880

Russell 1973: F. Russell, 'Portraits on the Grand Tour. Batoni's British Sitters', *Country Life*, vol. LIII, 7 June 1973, pp.1608-09

Russell 1975: F. Russell, 'Thomas Patch, Sir William Lowther and the Holker Claude', *Apollo*, vol. 102, August 1975, pp.115-19

Russell 1985: F. Russell, 'An early masterpiece by Carlo Dolci', *The Burlington Magazine*, vol. 77, no. 991, October 1985, p.716

Sala and Tarani 1929: T. Sala and F. Tarani, *Dizionario Storico Biografico dell'Ordine di Vallombrosa*, 2 vols., Florence 1929

Salerno 1963: L. Salerno, *Salvator Rosa*, Milan 1963

Sani 1988: *Rosalba Carriera*, Chieri (Turin) 1988

Siggins 1989: Lorna Siggins, 'Calling them obscene started it all', *The Irish Times*, Dublin, 2 February 1989

Steegman 1946: J. Steegman, 'Some English Portraits by Pompeo Batoni', *The Burlington Magazine*, March 1946, pp.55-63

Steegman 1933: J. Steegman, *Sir Joshua Reynolds*, London 1933

Strickland 1913: Walter G. Strickland, *A Dictionary of Irish Artists*, 2 vols., Dublin 1913

Sutton 1956: Denys Sutton, 'The Roman Caricatures of Reynolds', *Country Life Annual*, 1956, pp.115-17

Swift Maxims: Jonathan Swift, *Maxims Controlled in Ireland*, Prose Works, ed. H. Davis et al., 14 vols., Oxford 1939-1968

Tarraga Baldo 1992: M.L. Tarraga Baldo, *Giovan Domenico Olivieri y el Taller de Scultura del Palacio Real*, Madrid 1992

The Complete Peerage: G.E.C. *The Complete Peerage*, London 1932, enlarged by V. Gibbs

The Earl of Ilchester and Mrs Langford-Broke, *The Life of Sir Charles Hanbury-Williams*, London 1928

The Golden Age 1981: *The Golden Age of Naples: Art and Civilisation under the Bourbons, 1734-1805*, 2 vols., exhib. cat., Detroit Institute of Art and Chicago Art Institute, 1981

Thieme Becker: U. Thieme and F. Becker, *Allgemeines Lexikon der Bildenden Künstler*, Leipzig 1907

Ticozzi 1818: S. Ticozzi, *Dizionario dei Pittori del Rinnovamento delle Belle Arti fino al 1800*, Milan 1818

Topham Bowden 1791: Charles Topham Bowden, *A Tour through Ireland*, Dublin 1791

Turner 1996: Jane Turner (editor), *The Dictionary of Art*, Macmillan, London 1996

Twiss 1775: R. Twiss, *A Tour in Ireland*, 1775, 3rd edition, Dublin 1777

Valentine 1970: A. Valentine, *The British Establishment, 1760-1784*, Norman (Okla.) 1970

Venuti 1783: R. Venuti, 'Dissertazione sopra il gabinetto di Cicerone presentata alla nobile Accademia Etrusca di Cortona', pp.11-19, vol 2. of *Della Vita Privata de'Romani*, 2 vols. ed. by Domenico Amato, Naples 1783

Vertue 1810: G.W. Vertue, *A Dictionary of Painters, Sculptors Architects and Engravers*, London 1810

Vocabolario 1746: *Vocabolario degli Accademici della Crusca*, 5 vols., Naples 1746

Wallace 1967: R. Wallace, 'Salvator Rosa's "Death of Atilius Regulus", *The Burlington Magazine*, vol. 59, July 1967, pp.395-97

Walpole Correspondance: *Horace Walpole's Correspondence*, ed. W.S. Lewis et. al., 43 vols., New Haven & London 1937-1983

Ward Jackson 1958: Peter Ward Jackson, *English Furniture Designs of the Eighteenth Century*, London 1958

Waterhouse 1953: Eilis Waterhouse, *Painting in Britain 1530-1790*, New Haven & London 1953

Watson 1939-40: F.J.B. Watson, 'Thomas Patch (1725-1782): notes on his life together with a catalogue of his known works', *Walpole Society*, vol. 28, 1939-40, pp.16-50

Webster 1971: M. Webster, *Firenze e l'Inghilterra. Rapporti artistici e culturali del XVI al XX secolo*, exhib. cat., Florence 1971

White 1990: Elizabeth White (compiler), *Pictorial Dictionary of British 18th Century Furniture Design, the Printed Sources*, Woodbridge 1990

Wicklow Papers, National Library of Ireland

Wilton and Bignamini 1996: *Grand Tour: The Lure of Italy in the Eighteenth Century*, exhib. cat. ed. by Andrew Wilton and Ilaria Bignamini, Tate Gallery, London 1996

Wind 1949: Edgar Wind, 'A Source for Reynolds' Parody of "The School of Athens"', *Harvard Library Bulletin*, vol. III, no. 2, Spring 1949, pp.294-97

Wortley Montague Letters: *The complete letters of Lady Mary Wortley Montague*, ed. R. Halsband, 3 vols., Oxford 1965-67

Wood 1753: Robert Wood, *The Ruins of Palmyra*, London 1753

Wood 1757: Robert Wood, *The Ruins of Baalbec*, London 1757

Wright 1823: Rev. G.N. Wright, *Tours in Ireland or Guides to the Lakes of Killarney, the County of Wicklow and the Giants' Causeway. Illustrated Engravings after Drawings by G. Petrie*, London 1823

Wynne 1971: Michael Wynne, 'A Copy by Joseph Vernet of Salvator Rosa's "Atilius Regulus"', *The Burlington Magazine*, vol.113, September 1971, p.543

Wynne 1974: Michael Wynne, 'The Milltowns as Patrons, particularly concerning the picture-collecting of the first two Earls', *Apollo*, vol. 99, February 1974, pp.104-11

Wynne 1986: Michael Wynne, *Later Italian Paintings in The National Gallery of Ireland: The Seventeenth, Eighteenth and Nineteenth Centuries*, National Gallery of Ireland, Dublin 1986

Wynne 1990: Michael Wynne, 'Members from Great Britain and Ireland of the Florentine Accademia del Disegno 1700-1825', *The Burlington Magazine*, vol. 132, August 1990, pp.535-38

Wynne 1996[1]: Michael Wynne, 'Some British diplomats, some Grand Tourists and some students from Great Britain and Ireland in Turin in the eighteenth century', *Studi Piemontesi*, vol. 25, fasc. 1, March 1996, pp.145-60

Wynne 1996[2]: Michael Wynne, 'A Cache of Busiris' in *Hommage au Dessin-Mélanges offerts à Roseline Bacou*, Rimini 1996, pp.460-67

Index

(end notes are indicated in superscript; catalogue numbers in bold)

Adam, Robert, 24, 26, 56[12], 133
Aegean Islands, 26
Albani, Cardinal, 104
Alcibiades, 54
Apollo, 98
Aranjuez, Royal Palace, 100
Áras an Uachtaráin, 123[5]
Arch of Constantine, 48
Aristotle, 54
Athens, 26
Atilius Regulus, Marcus, 96

Baalbec, 26
Bagot, William, 56[10, 17]
Balestra, Antonio, 80
Baroque, 5
Barret, George, 5, 84
Barrett-Lennard, Thomas, 54, 55 (fig. 15), 56[8]
Batoni, Pompeo, 2, 3, 4, 12, 20[5], 21(**7**), 22, 23 (**8**), 24, 25 (**9**), 28, 29 (**11**), 30[2,4], 31 (**12**), 34, 50[10], 53 (figs.12-14), 55 (figs.15-17), 56[8, 9, 13], 100
Beit, Sir Alfred, 7, 78
Beit, Lady Clementine, 7
Belloni, Pietro, Don, 4, 5 (fig.3), 54[6], 78-79
Bellori, Giovanni Pietro, 51
Benedict XIII, Pope, 40, 102
Benson, Mr, 56[10]
Bernini, Gian Lorenzo, 37, 60, 71
Bindon, Francis, 2, 119
Bloemen, Jan van, 84
Borra, Giovanni Battista, 26
Bouverie, John, 26, 90[6]
Bracciano, 86
Brand, Thomas, 8[36]
Brettingham, Matthew, 54, 56[7], 104
Brice, Andrew, Dublin Alderman, 1, 12
Bridgewater, Francis Egerton, 3rd Duke of, 26
British, representative, 24
Bruce-Brudenell, Lord Thomas Baron of Tottenham, 38[4], 40, 41 (**15**), 42, 48, 49 (**18**), 50, 50[5], 54, 58 (**21**), 60, 60[5]
Busiri, Giovanni Battista, 84-87 (**29-32**)

Cacciatori, Carlo, 70
Callot, Jacques, 37
Canaletto, Antonio Canale called, 100
Carnival, 37, 51
Carracci, Annibale, 37
Carrara, 70
Carriera, Angela, 82
Carriera, Giovanna, 80
Carriera, Rosalba, 80-83 (**25-28**)
Carter, Thomas the younger, 120
Carton House, 32, 121, 123
Cassels or Castle, Richard, 2, 119, 120, 121
Castelgandolfo, 102
Castletown, Co. Kildare, 32[4], 123
Catiline, 98
Cavaceppi, Bartolomeo, 4, 104-105 (**46-47**)
Caulfield, see Charlemont, James, Lord, 3
Caulfield, Lord, son of Lord Charlemont, 50[8]
Chandler, Richard, 26
Charlemont, James, Lord, 3, 7[19], 8[24], (fig.13), 24, 38[4], 40, 43 (**16**), 42, 46, 48, 49 (**18**), 50, 50[9,10], 51 (fig.11), 54, 56[13,10], 58 (**22**), 60, 60[5]
Charles II, King, 1
Charles VII, King, 100
Chelsea, London, 6
Chippendale, Thomas, 121
Christine of Sweden, Queen, 104

Cicero, 106
Clanwilliam House, 120
Clement XI, Pope, 102
Clement XII, Pope, 104
Clements, Elizabeth Countess of Leitrim, 32, 32[4]
Clements, Robert Earl of Leitrim, 32
Clephane, Dr John, 20[4], 82, 94
Cloncurry, Valentine Lawless, 2nd Lord, 73[5]
Cole, Christian, 80
Collino, Ignazio, 71
Colonna Princes, 96
Commedia dell'Arte, 37
Conolly, Lady Louisa, 32[4]
Conolly, Thomas, 32[3]
Cook, Mr, 62, 65 (**22**)
Copeland, H., 122
Cortona, Pietro da, 114
Coypel, 80
Crozat, Pierre, 80

Daly, Capt. Denis, 67, 79[8], 123[15]
Damietta, 26
Dawkins, Henry, 26[10]
Dawkins, James, 26, 26[10], 82, 90[1]
Dawson, Judge Arthur, 7[8]
Dawson, Thomas, later Baron Dartrey and Vct Cremorne, 3, (fig. 20), 54, 56[13], 57 (fig. 20)
Devis, Arthur, 32
Diogenes, 54
Dody, see Joseph Leeson 2nd Earl of Milltown
Dolci, Carlo, 4, 100, 101[6]
Donacomper, Co. Kildare, 123[11]
Drake, William, 62, 65 (fig.22), 90[1]
Drogheda, St Peter's Church, 121
Dublin, 2, 24
Dublin Militia, 1
Dubois, Abbé, 54, 56[11]
Dubos, Jean-Baptiste, 56[11]
Dughet, Gaspar, 84

Emilia, 78
Eton, 22
Euclid, 54

Falconieri, Prince, 102
Fetherstonhaugh, Lady, 30[2]
Fetherstonhaugh, Sir Matthew, 53 (fig.14), 54, 54[6], 78, 90[6]
Fitzgerald, Emily Countess of Kildare later Duchess of Leinster, 8[27],32[4], 33[6]
Fitzgerald, James Earl of Kildare later Duke of Leinster, 8[27]
Florence, 4, 20, 24, 38, 50[9], 78, 110
Florence Court, 123
Foggini, Giovanni Battista, 98
Franceschi, Filippo, 101[6]
French, William, Revd, Dean of Armagh, 5, 34
French, aristocracy, 37
French, paintings, 6
French, privateer, 2
Furietti Centaurs, 2

Gallella, Gaetano, 114-15 (**55**)
Genoa, 70, 71
Ghetto degli Inglesi, 3
Ghezzi, Pier Leone, 7[21], 22, 22[5], 24, 24[3], 36 (fig.5), 37-38, 38 (fig.6), 40, 41 (**15**), 42, 45(figs.8-9), 46, 58, 62, 102-03
Giambologna, 110, 112
Girouette, 32[5]
Glasgow, 26

138

Glasnevin, Dublin, 7[13]
Glin Castle, Co. Limerick, 123[11]
Graeco-Roman, marble, 4
Grand Duke of Tuscany, 24
Grand Tour, 2, 4, 6, 20, 22, 24, 37, 46, 48, 72, 80, 132
Grand Tourists, 33[6], 37-38, 40
Gravelot, 121
Guarnacci, Mario, 102, 103 (fig.41)
Guarnieri Ottoni, Count Aurelio, 108[3]

Hades, 106
Hadrian's Villa, Tivoli, 2
Hamilton, Gavin, 26, 26[11], 27 (**10**)
Hamilton, Hugh Douglas, 32
Hanbury-Williams, Sir Charles, British Envoy, 50[4], 64[5]
Headfort, Co. Meath, 123[11]
Hermitage, Imperial Gallery, 70, 73[13]
Hervey, Capt. Augustus, 22[2]
Henry, Joseph, of Straffan 3-4, 7[18-19, 21], 10 (**9**), 22, 22[2], 24, 24[3], 25 (**9**), 36 (fig.5), 38, 40, 41 (**15**), 42, 44[9], 45 (figs.8-9), 46[1], 51, 54, 56[14], 58 (**21**), 60, 90, 100
Henry, Anne Leeson, of Straffan 2, 24
Henry, Hugh, Merchant and banker, 24
Herculaneum, 132
Hogarth, William, 16, 37
Holland, Lady, 33[6]
Houghton, John, 120, 121, 122, 123[6]
Howard, Ralph, of Shelton Abbey, later Earl of Wicklow, 7[18], 56[10, 13], 78, 79[6], 86[2], 98[6], 100, 101[3], 108[2], 150[10]
Huet, Mr, 62 (**23**)
Hugford, Don Enrico, 78
Hugford, Ignazio, 78
Hunter, Robert, 32, 33 (**13**)
Hunterian Museum, Glasgow, 26[10]
Huntingdon, Lord, 50[9]

Insurrection (1798), 6, 22
Ionian Islands, 26
Ireland, 4-5, 22
Iremonger, Lascelles, 54, 54[6], 55 (fig.16), 56[9]
Irish House of Commons, 2
Irish, portraitists, 16
Irwin, Dr, 54, 57 (fig.19), 56[12]
Italian, garden, 5

James I, 110
Jervas, Charles, 16
Joli, Antonio, 4, 24, 100-01 (**44**)
Jones, Inigo, 121
Juvara, Filippo, 71

Kelly, John, 120, 121, 122, 123[6]
Kennedy, Sir Thomas, 38 (fig.6), 48, 49 (**18**), 50[5], 51, 53 (fig.12) 58 (**22**), 60, 64[3]
Kerry, Lord, 32[5]
Kildare, County, 73[5]
Kildare, Lady, 122
Kilruddery, Co. Wicklow, 123[12]

Lafranchini, 5, 90[2], 120
Lancret, Nicolas, 116
Lee, Anthony, 14-15 (**3**), 16-17 (**4**), 18-19 (**5-6**)
Leeson, Anne Preston, Countess of Milltown, 2, 7[8], 20, 28
Leeson, Brice, 3rd Earl of Milltown, 1, 6
Leeson, Cecilia Leigh, 1, 2, 18-19 (**5**), 22
Leeson, Cecilia, daughter of the 1st Earl of Milltown, 34, 35 (**14**)
Leeson, Elizabeth French, Countess of Milltown, 5, 34, 35 (**14**)
Leeson, Geraldine Stanhope, Countess of Milltown, 7, 28, 73[1], 78, 79[9], 82, 105[7], 122
Leeson, Hugh, 1
Leeson, Joseph, of St Stephen's Green, 1, 7[2, 13], 12-13 (**1**), 14
Leeson, Joseph (1711?-1783), 1st Earl of Milltown, 1-2, 4-6, 7[1, 6, 13, 18], 8[24], 12, 14-15 (**3**), 16-17 (**4**), 18, 20[3, 5], 21 (**7**), 22, 22[2], 24, 26, 26[4], 28, 30[2], 34-35 (**14**), 38, 42, 52 (**19**), 54, 56[9], 58 (**20**), 60, 62 (**23**), 67, 72, 78, 80, 82, 84, 88, 89, 92, 94, 96, 98, 98[5], 100, 102, 104, 110, 119, 122, 123[1]
Leeson, Joseph (1730-1802), 2nd Earl of Milltown, 1, 3, 5-6, 8[27, 30], 22, 22[3, 5], 23 (**8**), 28, 32, 32[4-6], 33 (**13**), 33[6], 34, 38, 40, 42, 42 (fig.7), 43 (**16**), 46, 54, 58 (**21**), 60, 72, 110

Leeson Joseph, son of the 3rd Earl of Milltown, 34, 35 (**14**), 73[5]
Leeson, Margaret Brice, 1, 12-13 (**2**), 14
Leeson, Margaret, sister of Joseph Leeson, 1st Earl, 18, 30[2]
Leeson, Margaret (Peg Plunkett), 8[30], 12
Leeson, Mary, sister of Joseph Leeson, 1st Earl, 18
Leeson, Mary, daughter of the 1st Earl of Milltown, 28
Leeson, Martha, sister of Joseph Leeson, 1st Earl, 18
Leesons, 4-6, 8[36], 28, 46
Leeson, Fields, 1
Leeson, Walk, 1
Leigh, Francis of Rathangan, Co. Kildare, 18
Leinster, Duchess, Emily, 32[4]
Leinster, Duke, William, 32[4], 33[6]
Leinster House, 120
Lethieullier, Benjamin, 54, 54[6], 55 (fig.17), 56[9], 90[6]
Lethieullier, Sarah, 54[6]
Liffey, river, 5
Lint, Hendrick van, 84
Livorno, 51
Locatelli, Andrea, 78
Lock, Mathias, 121, 122, 123[11]
London, 2, 20, 40, 48
Lorrain, Claude, 50[9], 88
Lothario, 8[24], 68
Louis XIV, 100
Lowther, Sir William, 7[18], 48, 49 (**18**), 50[9], 54, 55 (fig. 18), 56[9], 58 (**20**), 60, 60[5], 62 (**23**)
Luti, Benedetto, 92
Lyttelton, Miss, 32[4]

Macartney, Mrs. 32[4]
Madrid, 73[22], 100
Malahide Castle, 123
Mann, Sir Horace, 24, 50[9]
Mannozzi, Giovanni, 'Giovanni da San Giovanni', 4
Mansell, Lord, 94
Mariette, 80
Marlay, Richard, Bishop of, 7[19], 8[24], 24, 68
Marseilles, 24
Martin, Charles, 4
Martin, John, 40, 41 (**15**), 42, 44[10]
Martin, Mrs, 32[5]
Martinez, Simone, 71
Maxwell, Robert, 56[10]
Medici, Francesco I de', 110
Medico, Count Carlo del, 70
Medusa, 106
Mengs, Anton Raphael, 26
Merrion Street, upper, 34
Midleton, Lord George Brodrick, 40, 41 (**15**), 42
Milles, Dr Jeremiah, 7[14]
Milltown Earl, 1st, see Leeson Joseph
Milltown Earl, 2nd, see Leeson Joseph
Milltown Earl, 3rd, see Leeson Brice
Milltown Earls, 1, 6, 106
Minorca, 51
Modena, 100
Moira, 1st Earl, 24
Mondovì, 71
Murphy, Revd Edward, 54, 56[15]
Muti, Marchesi, 50[9]

Naples, 22[2], 26, 74, 75, 76, 100
National Gallery of Ireland, 7[20], 28, 40
National Portrait Gallery, London, 26
Newbridge, Co. Dublin, 123
Newcome William, Archbishop of Armagh, 34
Newton, Jonathan, 128
Nugent, Edward, 6th Earl of Milltown, 72[1]

Olivieri, Giovanni Domenico, 70, 71, 73[22]
Odescalchi, Prince, 104

Padua, 26
Palmyra, 26

139

Pancrazi, Giuseppe Maria, 22[2]
Panini, Giovanni Paolo, 2, 40, 82, 92-93 (**37-40**), 100
Parma, Duca di, 40
Parodi, Filippo, 70, 71
Patch, Thomas, 38, 38[4], 48, 50, 50[9], 54, 56[14], 90
Pater, Jean-Baptiste, 116
Pergamon, 98
Phelps, Richard, 51, 53, 58 (**22**), 60
Philadelphia, 40
Philip V, 104
Piacenza, 92
Piamontini, Giovanni Battista, 4, 98-99 (**42-43**), 108[2]
Piamontini, Giuseppe, 98
Piazza di Spagna, 22, 40
Piazza Navona, 40
Pilkington Letitia, 1-2, 7, 123[1]
Pisa, 24
Plato, 54
Plunkett, Peg, see Leeson, Margaret
Pocock, Bishop, 8[26]
Polignac, Cardinal Melchior de, 40
Pompeii, 132
Pond, Arthur, 37
Ponsanelli, Giacomo Antonio, 70
Poulaphouca, falls and reservoir, 5
Powerscourt House, 123
Privy Council of Ireland, 5
Provost House, 123
Puget, Pierre, 70, 71

Ramsay, Allan, 26
Raphael, 3, 51, 54, 100, 114
Rathcormack, Co. Cork, 2
Rathcormick (Rathcormack), 2
Rawdon, Lady Catherina, 24
Read, John Othan, 129
Royal Academy, Turin, 22, 22[3], 33[6]
Reni, Guido, 114
Restoration, The, 131
Revett, Nicholas, 26
Reynolds, Joshua, 3, 7[18], 24, 38, 42, 48, 51-65 (**19-23**, figs.18, 21, 22), 50[11],100
Riverstown Castle, 26
Roisecco, Gregorio, 42
Rome, 2, 3, 20, 22, 24, 34, 37, 42, 48, 50[9, 10], 51, 56, 68, 71, 74, 80, 84, 86, 88, 90, 92, 96, 100, 102, 104, 114
Rosa, Salvator, 2, 88, 96
Rowe, Nicholas, 4
Ruslen, John, 130
Russborough, 2-4, 6, 7[17], 8[26, 27], 20[7], 23[8], 28, 66 (fig.23), 67-73 (figs.24-27), 78, 82, 84, 88, 90[2], 119-123 (figs. 43, 44)
Russborough, Lord, see Joseph Leeson (1711?-1783)
Russborough, Lord, see Joseph Leeson (1730-1802)
Russell, James, 50, 108[4]
Russellsborough (Russborough), 2, 20
Russellstown, 2, 20

Sabbatini, M. Antonio, 64[14]
Salamon Collection, 112
San Gillio, Contessa, 33[6]
Savoy, Charles Emmanuel III, 4th Duke of , 71, 73[16]
Seneca, 106, 108[2]
Sermoneta, Duchess, 30[2]
Siena, 62
Silenus, 114
Singleton, Lord Chief Justice Henry, 108[2]
Slaughter, Stephen, 16
Soane, Sir John, Museum, 62
Society of Dilettanti, 5, 26, 50[4]
Socrates, 54

Sodoma, Giovanni Antonio Bazzi called il, 54, 56[14]
Solari, Bartolomeo, 70, 71, 72, 73[7, 22], 74-76 (figs.28-40)
Solari, Stefano, 71, 73[22]
Spanish Steps, 3
St Gille, Madame, 33[6]
St James'Church, Westminster, London, 6
St Peter and St. Kevin, Church, Dublin, 1
St Stephen's Green, North, (Dublin), 5, 34
St Stephen's Green, South, (Dublin), 1, 14, 16
Steavens,Thomas, 48, 49 (**18**) (fig.10), 50[4, 9-10], 56[9], 64[5]
Sterling, Mr, 54
Stosch, Baron Philip von, 64[4]
Straffan, Co. Kildare, 24
Stuart, James 'Athenian', 26
Sweetman, Patrick, brewer, 7[11]
Swift, Jonathan, Dean of St Patrick, 1, 7[2], 119

Tacca, Ferdinando, 110-13 (**51-54**)
Tacca, Pietro, 110
Tagus, river, 100
Tassi, Agostino, 88
Thomas, Edward, 2, 7[14]
Ticinesi, 5
Tiepolo, Gianbattista, 37
Tiepolo, Giandomenico, 37
Tivoli, 2, 3, 86, 104
Trotter, J., 56[7]
Tully, 108[2]
Turin, 71, 72
Turner, Charles of Kirkleatham, 38[4],48, 49 (**18**), 50, 62 (**23**)
Turton, Sir Edmund R., 79[8], 122, 123[13]
Tyrone House, 120
Tyrrell, Dr James, 56[13], 98, 98[5, 6], 101[3], 106, 108[2]
Twiss, Richard, 100

Uffizi, Tribuna, 4, 75, 76, 98, 110
Ulster, 32
Uppark, Sussex, 78

Valentini, Domenico, 64[3]
Venice, 4, 7[21], 26, 37, 80, 100
Venuti, Ridolfo, 108[3]
Vernet, Claude-Joseph, 2, 4, 24, 26[4], 54[6], 56[9, 13, 14], 82, 89-91 (**33-36**), 96-97 (**41**), 100
Versailles, 100
Victoria and Albert Museum, 122
Vierpyl, Simon, 54, 56[7]
Viscount Russborough and Russellstown (Joseph Leeson 1711?-1783), 5
Viscount Russborough and Russellstown (Joseph Leeson 1730-1802), 5
Vleughels, Nicolas, 88

Wallace Collection, 112
Ward, John, 38 (fig.6), 58 (**22**), 60
Watteau, Antoine, 80, 116
West, James of Alscot Park, 50[4]
Wexford, County, 67
Wickes, George, 119, 122
Wicklow, County, 2, 67, 78, 122
Wilson, Richard, 3, 7[20], 24, 100
Wittel, Gaspard van, 84
Wood, Richard of Summerhill, Co. Meath, 26
Wood, Robert, 2, 26, 26[3], 27 (**10**), 82, 90
Woodyeare, John, 7[18], 62, 65 (fig.22)
Wortley Montague, Lady Mary, 60[5]

Yale, 42

Zanetti, Antonio Maria, 37
Zocchi, Giuseppe, 78

Photography Credits: Photography by Roy Hewson except nos. 9, 15, 16, 18 and figs. 5-10 and 12-22.